DATA
CULTURE

DATA CULTURE

How to Succeed with Digital Transformation and Artificial Intelligence

Alex Vail

ICON

Published in the UK in 2025 by
Icon Books Ltd, Omnibus Business Centre,
39–41 North Road, London N7 9DP
email: info@iconbooks.com
www.iconbooks.com

ISBN: 978-183773-231-9
ebook: 978-183773-230-2

Typeset by SJmagic DESIGN SERVICES, India

Printed and bound in Great Britain

Appointed GPSR EU Representative: Easy Access System Europe Oü, 16879218
Address: Mustamäe tee 50, 10621, Tallinn, Estonia
Contact Details: gpsr.requests@easproject.com, +358 40 500 3575

Contents

Introduction

Like so many great ideas, it started with cocktails...

Picture the scene: two friends, who have worked together on and off for the last twelve years, are sitting in a fancy cocktail bar in Greenwich Village, New York City. It's early May, an unseasonably warm New York evening and local residents stroll past the window in T-shirts and shorts, lost in their own worlds as their designer dogs stop to sniff the last of the cherry blossom on the sidewalk.

I had been made redundant the previous week along with the rest of my team, when Series B funding for the AI innovation startup I was working in fell through. My friend Michella, a very smart woman, did the responsible thing and booked us both cheap flights from Heathrow to the Big Apple for a few days, so I could regroup and plan next steps.

Perched on high stools in the cocktail bar, as our feet throbbed from the 15 miles we'd walked that day around Manhattan and Central Park, she asked me a series of leading questions, as if interviewing me for my future. I talked about the anguish I felt about having had to lay off such a talented team. I explained how grateful I was that I'd had a chance to work with such a visionary CEO and how disappointed our clients had been that some of our really exciting transformation projects would never come to fruition. But most of all, I spoke about how much I had learned in the role. After 25 years of working across several industries which were struggling with the onslaught of new technologies – where it had been clear that no one seemed able to succeed with digital transformation – I had finally been able to understand, and help companies solve, the root causes of transformation failure.

For the last year and a half, I had been in the eye of the storm, spending time with Chief Technology Officers (CTOs), Chief Information Officers (CIOs), Heads of Data Strategy and data innovation experts, talking about the problems their old-world industrial and services businesses experienced in trying to keep pace with technological change.

Automotive, manufacturing, law, banking, pharmaceutical, precision engineering, healthcare, aerospace, defence... regardless of which sector they worked in, every single one of them had faced the same struggles as they tried to reverse-engineer artificial intelligence (AI), machine learning (ML) and data science into well-established, complex, process-driven environments, to secure the future of their businesses.

They were all using emerging technologies in different ways, for different purposes, but their challenges were precisely the same, because it wasn't the technology that was the problem. They were all operating in cultures which rejected AI transformations for the same reasons that digital transformations the world-over have consistently failed in companies for more than thirty years.

They needed a data-driven culture. And they didn't know how to create one. The human problem felt insurmountable.

'Are you telling me,' Michella asked incredulously, 'that you finally managed to *solve* digital transformation?'

'I think so,' I replied. 'We were dangerously close to proving it. If we'd just had another couple of months ...'

'Then when we get back to London, it seems like you have two choices about what to do next,' she said, matter-of-factly.

'Either you draw a line under it, chalk it up to experience and find another job ...'

I took another sip of my margarita and considered this while we watched the dog walkers outside the window. 'Or? What's the alternative?'

'Keep on digging in. Prove it,' she shrugged, with a glint in her eye.

That was how I found myself, back in London a week later, launching the first pieces of research that would eventually lead to this book.

I made a few calls and asked for help from a couple of friends who worked in different research agencies and knew each other socially. They challenged me to be clear on what question I was trying to answer. I told them that previous clients had clear struggles with data and with digital culture. We came up with the following challenge statement:

Can we pull together enough data points and expert opinions to prove my earlier anecdotal evidence, that barriers to digital transformation are common, pervasive, complex and cultural?

Once we'd established the research 'mission', we segmented my professional network into 'technology people' and 'sustainability people' and they helped me build two concurrent research projects:

1. A qualitative survey with board members and senior executives in businesses which had made Net Zero pledges, to identify the complexity of their management information (MI) and the importance for them of being able to understand and interpret sustainability data.
2. Qualitative interviews with senior innovation, change and transformation leaders about implementing digital culture change in large businesses.

Over the next five weeks, I carried out deep-dive interviews with 22 leaders on the culture question and the online survey received 105 responses. The data told a really interesting story, but halfway through the project, I realised we'd missed a trick by not targeting CTOs and CIOs, and really 'zeroing in' on the broader challenges around digital transformation and implementing new technology.

I needed to speak to the problem owners. So in June 2023, two new studies were launched:

1. Qualitative interviews with CTOs, CIOs and Chief Data or Digital Officers in major global corporates about challenges implementing Software-as-a-Service (SaaS) solutions at-scale.
2. A survey with CIOs, CTOs and AI directors in enterprise-scale businesses, exploring the business risks and barriers around digital transformation.

The respondent pool was a little more niche, but the 17 interviews I carried out and 38 survey respondents completely fit the profile we were looking for: these were very senior people in really big companies and their feedback was invaluable. Once a pattern emerged in the responses around a set of challenges with digital talent, skills and culture, I held the first round table, kindly hosted by one of the earliest participants and involving several of the earlier interviewees, to dig a little deeper into the problem. A structured, but free-flowing discussion provided a huge amount of context and insight into one of the biggest problems they all expressed frustration about: that their chief executives, boards and executive teams didn't have a great level of understanding when it came to data strategy. That round table also started to build a community which would be the foundation stone of what came next.

Moving into July, I asked our previous interviewees and participants to introduce me to the people they most wanted me to talk to:

1. I carried out 16 interviews with non-executive directors (NEDs), Company Secretaries, Chairs, board advisors and management consultants, about the current state of play with executive data literacy.
2. I held 11 interviews with senior governance professionals and management consultants, to dig deeper into the earlier study about trends in MI and board reporting.
3. Finally, I held a round table in London with some of the interviewees, to discuss their perspectives on data risks and reporting.

Context is critical and it is worth noting that all of these research projects were taking place against a media backdrop in which AI was in the news on a regular basis. With the launch of ChatGPT in November 2022 and the widespread coverage capturing the public discourse around the rise of artificial intelligence – and generative AI in particular – many of the discussions touched on its real or perceived impacts. Certainly, the view from many board members I spoke to was that AI would be the biggest technological change their businesses had faced in decades.

One thing that was consistent with the interviewees was the sense that AI development was an arms race that everyone suspected they might be losing, often to their direct market competitors. For competitive reasons, companies tend not to reveal levels of investment or tech development publicly, so this burgeoning community told me it would be helpful if there was a benchmarking study, to identify which sectors were leading the pack, so that at least they could begin to understand what 'good' looked like.

So, in August 2023, I launched a new project, to better understand this issue:

1. I conducted 26 interviews with senior executives (heads of, VPs, directors & C-suite) about their corporate AI capabilities, talent, skills and investment.

2. I polled 91 senior leaders (CEOs, chairs, NEDs, C-suite, directors, heads of) about corporate AI, machine learning and data science capabilities in the large businesses they worked in.

Several months into the research, featuring 92 in-person and virtual interviews, three round tables and 234 survey responses from across every market segment, capturing the views of hundreds of market-leading organisations, I could now comfortably say that I had met the original challenge statement by gathering 'enough data points and expert opinions to prove my earlier anecdotal evidence, that barriers to digital transformation are common, pervasive, complex and cultural'.

Not only that, but the depth and quality of those conversations helped me to identify some very clear common executive-level barriers, and what is needed for organisations to overcome them.

1. **Most business leaders don't understand data, or how to unlock value from it.**

   - Just 23% of CEOs, executives and board members understand and trust the data they make strategic decisions with;
   - Only one in five CTOs believes their Executive Committee (Exco) and board has the skills and culture to deliver their digital strategy;
   - Fewer than 4% of board members and 9% of executive leaders in UK PLCs are perceived to have any technology background or experience;
   - 58% of large firms do not have an AI expert in the top three tiers of management.

2. **Poor communication between experts and executives leads to data strategy failure.**

   - Lack of executive data literacy and poor data strategy account for nearly a third of transformation risks;

- 87% of senior executives and board members feel that MI has become more complex over the previous three years;
- 78% of leaders say they expect to be 'largely' or 'completely' reliant on data to make decisions in the next two years.

This book tells the story of how, with a willing band of volunteers, we began to create a new kind of global peer-learning and research network for senior technology executives, to help them address these problems: a truly collaborative community of transformational changemakers, who are learning to help themselves, their companies and each other, to adopt new ways of working and communicating. By recognising common barriers and supporting each other, these pioneers are actively developing workplace cultures where humans understand how data can help them to do more, faster, better.

As companies become more reliant on interpreting and understanding data, it has never been more essential to break down communications barriers between technology professionals and senior managers, to influence change in their organisations. In my role as a board advisor and professional career coach, I work with data experts and senior executives, to help them find ways to communicate more effectively, navigate conflict, manage upwards and ask the right questions.

With collaborative peer-to-peer communities, providing opportunities for professionals to share knowledge and best practice, leaders have a chance to work together, communicate more effectively, recruit and retain technical talent, build more inclusive and responsible AI and embed resilient data cultures in their organisations.

Over the next few years, data will continue to rise in prominence in corporate risk registers. Drawing on the extensive body of research in this book, and working with our community of domain experts and problem owners, I have developed a set of cultural principles, laid out as a comprehensive list of 44 'Elements', and distilled those into a practical action plan for leaders to follow, all in Part Three. Collectively, these identify the most consistent behaviours and attributes that experts say are the most likely indicators of digital transformation success.

Spoiler alert: this book isn't really about technology. It's about people. More specifically it's about how you can help humans in your organisation adapt to transformation programmes, minimising the risk of 'corporate tissue rejection'.

I hope you enjoy Part One, which explores thirty years' worth of research into why most digital transformations fail. Part Two, which I hope you find enlightening, explores the biggest current transformation challenge facing most businesses: how to unlock value from artificial intelligence... and why most businesses will fail to unlock value return from their AI investments, for the same reasons they tend to fail with all digital transformation.

However, most of the actionable value of the book is in Part Three, where you will find the **Periodic Table of Data Strategy Elements** and the **Data Success Framework**: two resources designed from a great deal of work and research, which should provide you with an easy-to-follow set of principles and actions to turn transformation into a positive process of necessary change.

The Framework helps business leaders to: understand the cultural, communications and development risks they have around data; identify and engage high-potential talent; benchmark their cultural and strategic data capabilities; build measurable action plans for success; and embed a culture where AI and other data-driven technologies thrive.

This book is also an attempt to collate all of the incredible insights from across different industries, bringing together voices from some of the world's most impressive experts and companies, to identify the root causes of digital transformation failure, to paint a clear picture of where we are right now, where we are headed, what the challenges and risks are, and to make some clear recommendations for anyone designing, building or just living through a business change programme.

I hope you find it *transformative*.

PART ONE

Why
transformations fail

1

A short history of digital transformation

If you don't include the fruit and veg shop where I had my Saturday job as a teenager, or the river piers I worked on in my summer holidays, I have spent 25 years in the workplace. The positions I have held and the companies I've worked in have varied but they were all office jobs. From my first full time role as the office junior, to C-suite and board positions, all these jobs would these days be referred to as part of the 'knowledge economy'.

All of these roles would now be subject to disruption from the rapid rise of artificial intelligence, some of them with the same devastating effect that my mother's profession was, following the launch of Microsoft's Windows 95. You see, my mum was a typesetter, which involved her taking other people's words and laying them out beautifully in book form. This was a very specialised skill set which, thanks to Bill Gates's pledge to put 'a PC on every desk and in every home', has become more a vocation for the few than a profession for the many in the intervening years. As a child in the 1980s, I remember helping my mum change fonts, an elaborate process which involved ejecting the Helvetica cartridge from the hard drive and replacing it with a Garamond cartridge. The enormous orange Quadritek 1200 computer she worked on in the spare bedroom was the pinnacle of word processing technology in 1979, because you could plug in up to four fonts at a time! Mum moved with the times and upgraded by investing in an astronomically expensive Apple Macintosh computer in 1994, but her entire business model was almost extinct ten years later.

The timing of my working life also means that I've had a front row seat at the theatre of digital transformation for 25 years. This has taken many forms, and they haven't all been grand enough to call them 'change programmes', but from launching companies' first websites and apps, to migrating conflicting CRM systems, to 'digitising' tens of thousands of paper records (we now all realise that scanning and PDFing was *really not* digitising anything!), to bringing together the disparate systems and processes of all entities in a six-way merger... managing change has formed a significant chunk of, and persistent drumbeat to, my career.

Most companies are doomed to failure when it comes to unlocking value from artificial intelligence, for the same reasons they tend to fail at all types of digital transformation. So in this chapter, we will explore what those reasons are, and what can be done to reduce the failure rate of change programmes.

During June 2023, while carrying out an industry survey of CTOs, CIOs and technology leaders about their own digital transformation experiences, I also conducted a meta-review of hundreds of surveys, thought leadership reports and research papers from academics, consulting firms and trade bodies, to establish the current state of play, levels of technology investment and common problems of businesses facing into data-driven business change programmes.

Given the seismic impact the pandemic had (and is still having) on ways of working in just about every business in the world, I read with interest – but largely discounted – any research pre-dating Covid-19 and focused the review instead on research and content published since 2020.

The most-often cited statistic on this issue in the last few years (which almost everyone I spoke to took as gospel) is the Boston Consulting Group finding from 2020 that 70% of digital transformations fail, often because of a lack of cultural readiness.[1]

Since then, many thousands of business leaders in every industry sector have been quizzed on how their businesses operate, and how their past or present data transformation programmes have fared. Here are some of the key statistics from that review, grouped loosely into three categories: culture and skills, leadership, and the pace of technological change...

Culture and skills

29% of CEOs rate 'scarcity and cost of talent with the right skills to accelerate growth' in their top three greatest business risks – *EY, 2023*

24% of global technology leaders rank risk-averse cultures in their top five digital-transformation challenges – *KPMG, 2022*

73% of employers believe their current workforce does not have the necessary skill set to deliver on their digitalisation strategy – *Eversheds Sutherland, 2022*

Two-thirds (67%) of employees say opportunities to learn new skills are a key factor in any decision to job-switch – *PwC, 2024*

'Lack of capable digital talent' was cited as the most common obstacle to the adoption of new technologies – *KPMG, 2022*

72% of business leaders say improving organisational agility is a strategic priority – *PA Consulting, 2022*

71% of major corporates have low levels of data literacy and competency – *Capgemini Research Institute, 2022*

67% of senior leaders have experienced at least one underperforming transformation since 2017 – *EY, 2022*

'Finding enough employees with critical skills' was cited as the most common workforce issue for leaders – *Alix Partners, 2022*

47% of business leaders struggle to attract and reskill tech-savvy executive talent – *McKinsey & Company, 2022*

Leadership

83% of CEOs say their board of directors impedes the process of adopting essential new technology solutions – *Alix Partners, 2022*

80% of business leaders complain that their senior leadership's risk aversion means their organisation is slower than competitors to embrace new technology – *KPMG, 2024*

80% of business executives do not trust the data they receive to make decisions with – *Capgemini Research Institute, 2022*

45% of CEOs believe their company won't be viable in 10 years if it stays on its current path – *PwC, 2024*

Just 20% of businesses have corporate digital responsibility ownership and oversight at board-level – *Eversheds Sutherland, 2020*

'Executives were too scared or simply unwilling to learn the digital skills they needed or to embrace their evolving role within the organisation' – *EY, 2020*

72% of CEOs say their executive team lacks the agility to deal with impending disruption – *Alix Partners, 2022*

52% of executives feel that in the next five years their biggest competitor will be a startup or 'digital native' company – *Deloitte, 2021*

53% of senior executives have identified data and analytics as their top investment priority in the next two years – *EY, 2022*

85% of CEOs say it has become increasingly difficult to know what to prioritise – *Alix Partners, 2022*

57% of C-suite respondents cite lack of buy-in from senior leadership as holding them back from improving interoperability – *Accenture, 2022*

9 in 10 digital leaders say they still need to get better at helping the board understand the potential of new technologies – *KPMG, 2023*

The pace of technological change

78% of business leaders worry they are struggling to keep up with the pace of change – *KPMG, 2024*

52% of executives feel the fast pace of technology change is not good for their company or their customers – *Deloitte, 2021*

69% of operations and supply chain leaders say tech investments haven't fully delivered expected results – *PwC, 2024*

95% of global executives believe next-generation computing will be a major driver of breakthroughs in their industry over the next decade – *Accenture, 2023*

63% of CEOs say their company cannot keep up with the pace of technology advancements – *Alix Partners, 2024*

Just 14% of UK business leaders feel confident in their ability to pivot, augment or retrofit their digital technologies quickly to comply with changes in applicable law – *Eversheds Sutherland, 2022*

79% of leaders are concerned about the proliferation of 'dark data' but are unsure how to approach the issue – *Accenture, 2022*

96% of executives agree that the convergence of digital and physical worlds over the next decade will transform their industry – *Accenture 2023*

85% of tech leaders feel major change is happening faster than ever and are worried about economic disruption – *CIONET, 2022*

And, interestingly, in a new statistic to challenge the BCG gospel that 70% of digital transformations fail, McKinsey & Company found in 2023 that only 12% of transformation programmes achieve their performance goals and sustain them for more than three years.

Many of these statistics proved to be useful talking points in discussion groups and interviews with chief technology and information officers during the *Barriers to Digital Transformation* research study, in which I carried out:

(a) qualitative interviews with CTOs, CIOs and CDOs in major global corporates about the challenges implementing SaaS solutions and new technologies at-scale; and

(b) an online survey with CIOs, CTOs & AI Directors in enterprise-scale businesses, exploring the business risks and barriers around digital transformation.

While this research sample was relatively small, with 38 survey respondents, 17 in-person or virtual interviews and one round table discussion group, the calibre of participants (who were not anonymous) was incredibly high, with 92% of them self-identifying as 'problem-owners', in the top three tiers of management. This sample was from large organisations: enterprise firms which had an average of 26,800 full-time employees in their UK entities.

Have you experienced a failed digital transformation in the last five years?

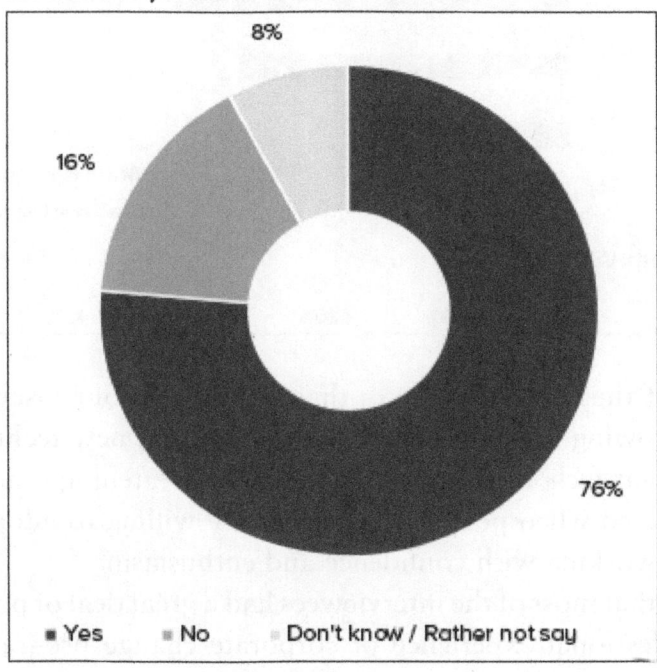

8%

16%

76%

■ Yes   ■ No   Don't know / Rather not say

In the survey, I asked respondents whether they had experienced a failed digital transformation in the last five years. Over three quarters (76%) said they had, while only 16% said they had not, with nearly one in ten saying they didn't know or would prefer not to say.

Technology leaders told me they lacked confidence that their workforce had the necessary culture and skills to deliver on their company's digital strategy, with 86% expressing low confidence levels.

Some CTOs, CIOs and AI Directors expressed greater confidence in their executive team and board, but one in five also expressed no confidence at all.

With 0 representing no confidence and 5 representing full confidence, how confident are you that your workforce / executive team and Board members has the necessary culture and skills to deliver on your company's digital strategy?

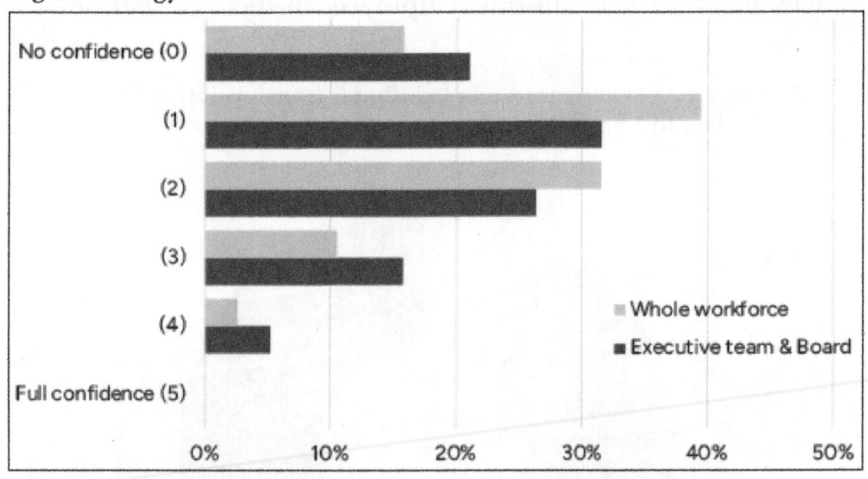

One of the consistent issues that came up in our discussions was a growing recognition among leaders that new technology deployment feels disruptive – sometimes threatening – and can only succeed when people at all levels are willing to adopt new ways of working with confidence and enthusiasm.

Given that most of the interviewees had a great deal of personal and professional experience of corporate change programmes,

I asked them to identify the most likely and least likely indicators they look for in a successful data transformation strategy. The questions I asked this group – and the answers they provided – formed the bedrock of months of discussion and collaboration, which would eventually lead to the Periodic Table of Data Strategy Elements and the Data Success Framework, which are explained in Part Three.

The majority of CTOs, CIOs and technology leaders agreed that 'aligning the transformation with the overall business strategy' was the most important *strategic* priority, while 'leading with empathy and kindness' was the most important *people* priority. Taken in aggregate, the most successful indicators of a data transformation programme can be mapped as follows:

Where 1 is least likely and 5 is most likely, please rank the following strategy / people priorities as the most likely indicators of a successful digital transformation

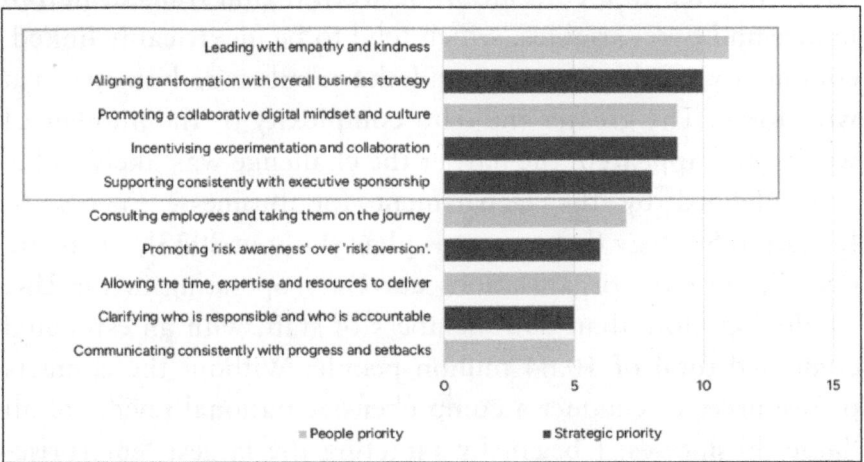

What does the digital transformation market look like?

The need for businesses to adapt to constant technological change is near universal. While my desk research focused on the 400 biggest businesses in the UK, most of which tend to skew older, during the course of writing this book I have spoken to organisations of all sizes, in all industries and all ages. The smallest and youngest company – where I interviewed the CEO – had fewer than 30 members of staff, was less than a decade old and actively works in the emerging technology space. And she told me even they have invested over £200,000 in the last year on a digital transformation programme which is proving to be incredibly difficult to deliver.

The studies carried out over many months focused on the biggest firms with the most complex requirements, on the premise that it is better to develop solutions that work across all challenge areas and scale them down, as required, to meet fewer levels of complexity, than it is to design them for fewer challenge areas before attempting to scale up accordingly.

Digital transformation is an incredibly lucrative industry on its own. Almost every professional services, IT, technology or consulting firm seems to offer services to help identify and solve business change problems.

I began the research from a baseline of anecdotal evidence which pointed to a correlation between digital transformation failure and two variables, which tend to be inextricably linked: complexity of data sources and the number of humans in a workforce. The greater the data complexity or the number of workers, it appeared, the harder the challenge was likely to be.

As defined by the Department for Business, Energy & Industrial Strategy (before it was phased out in 2023),[2] there are over 7,700 large organisations currently operating in the UK, employing more than 250 members of staff, with an estimated combined total of 10.64 million people. Without the contacts or resources to conduct a comprehensive national review of all 'large' businesses, I began by targeting the largest 'enterprise-scale' companies, by reviewing FTSE and other UK stock market listings, annual reports, investor websites and publicly available data to identify the 437 businesses in the UK with the highest revenues from 2022 (or in some cases, 2021). I excluded from the research a small number of hedge funds and other (mostly financial services) firms with far fewer than 250 staff, so that the sample consisted of large employers.

The remaining 400 business I focussed on - mostly enterprise-scale, employing more than 1,000 people - are headquartered in, or have a major presence in, the UK. These companies employ 8.11m people in the UK (26% of the workforce) and are most likely to be dealing with extensive legacy infrastructure, the result of decades of growth, mergers and acquisitions, which provides inherent data complexity issues.

On average, these firms are 107 years old, employ 28,613 people each and spend an estimated £13.5m per year on technology R&D. The top 250 UK-headquartered companies (by revenue) have combined revenues of $1.927.5tn, approximately 55% of the UK's GDP.

Of the 400 largest employers in the UK, 89% are older than the internet. More of them pre-date the Industrial Revolution than have been established since the birth of the web. These are multi-generational companies, with shareholders, tens of thousands of employees and – culturally at least – they are looking further ahead than the standard five-year business strategy. Many of these businesses are investing in new technologies with the same enthusiasm their predecessors brought to electrification. They plan to be around at the turn of the next century. And the one after that.

Date of establishment of the UK's largest 400 companies

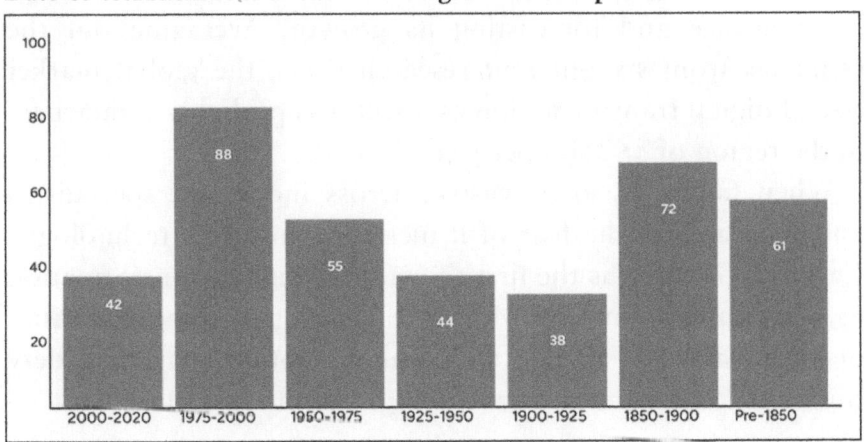

These companies have not survived without change. They have adapted, merged, acquired and evolved. Many processes have had to be updated but inevitably, some have stayed the same for generations, with ways of working passed from manager to apprentice. For some of their workers through the years, the introduction of the computer may have seemed like a passing fad.

Each of these organisations holds personal, business, sensitive and behavioural data on thousands or millions of customers worldwide. Each one is the custodian of billions or trillions of proprietary data points, hidden in silos, from complex schematics and patented technology, to ground-breaking IP and detailed intelligence on international supply systems.

The 358 companies in the market research sample which were founded before the 21st century are the most likely customers for such services, as they don't have digital technologies baked into their DNA. There can be found a corresponding range of solution providers for any business, regardless of what stage they are at on their journey, to help reverse-engineer existing business models into successful data-driven organisations.

Digital transformation is such a big marketplace that there is even a thriving cottage industry devoted to estimating its growing size and forecasting its growth. Averaging out the estimates from six different research firms, the global market size of digital transformation as a sector is probably somewhere in the region of $625bn per year.

When failure is so pervasive, across industries, specialisms and geographies, the fear of it increases. In 2022, technologist Caroline Gorski was the first to compare digital transformation to what author Timothy Morton called 'hyper-objects': entities of such vast spatial and temporal disruption that they defy traditional ideas about what a thing is in the first place.

So when I started talking to business leaders, collecting the views of over 300 organisations, I found they were beginning to see transformation not as a problem that could be solved, but as a set of symptoms which at best could be managed. This limiting of aspiration from business leaders may in itself be one of the symptoms: EY found in 2022 that 67% of senior leaders have experienced at least one underperforming transformation since 2017.

Because so many of them already bear the scars of failure, the expectation most senior executives and board members now have of consulting firms working in this space has shifted accordingly. One interviewee, a Chief Data Officer in a high street retailer, compared his company's evolving relationship with a Big Four consulting firm to preparing his village's flood defences: 'We used to ask them to build a better river wall, but the water kept rising, so now they make us the best sandbags and waterproof our furniture instead.'

This growing sense of failure being inevitable eventually corrodes morale at every level: as EY found, 50% of workers who experienced an underperforming transformation agreed that 'transformation' was just another word for 'layoffs'. Speaking with leaders across finance, healthcare, engineering, pharmaceutical, energy and other sectors, I have discovered that no industry is immune and everyone is facing the same challenges:

1. **Most business leaders don't understand data, or how to unlock value from it.**
   AI seems to be in the news every day, but business-relevant insight is rare, so the vast majority of decision-makers don't really understand what data-driven technologies might mean for them, their organisations, their people or their bottom lines. Limited educational support means boards and executive teams struggle to make well-informed decisions around AI, machine learning and data strategy. Consequently,

the lack of executive support and understanding hinders most transformation programmes.

2. **Poor communication between experts and executives leads to data strategy failure.**
   New technology deployment feels disruptive and threatening and can only succeed when people at all levels approach new ways of working with confidence and enthusiasm. Adapting old ways to new technology doesn't always feel intuitive and successful cultural change requires adoption of a number of incremental changes to mindset and behaviours. Embedding a digital culture requires a willingness to collaborate and communicate.

This book will hopefully help you see that those two pervasive challenges are intertwined and completely solvable. Transformation is never easy, but it is fulfilling, and it can be done. My hope is to help you understand three things by reading this:

1. How you can help the humans who are at the core of any transformation programme;
2. Why businesses put up barriers to innovation and how you can overcome them;
3. How, using AI and data transformation, you can unlock the value that is hiding in plain sight.

2

Transformation vs. the 100-year business plan

For most organisations, technology isn't a core product, it's an enabler, and the priority – understandably if you're in a tightly regulated sector, like healthcare, banking or defence – is going to be the compliance, security and the safety of your customers, patients, passengers or employees.

Businesses became enterprise-scale over time by being very good at making or selling things, so technology advancements over the last couple of decades have enabled them to make those things faster, or sell them more effectively. Consequently, these companies often occupy monopolistic or oligopolistic market positions and their products are made, marketed, sold and shipped globally, touching people in every household or workplace in the world.

It is often difficult to communicate the importance of data strategies effectively to the people running those organisations. Not only are they rarely 'digital natives', with the intuitive sense of those who have grown up with internet-enabled technologies, but also because of their very real subject matter expertise. They usually reach senior leadership positions because they are experts in their fields, whether that's in manufacturing, energy, automotive or hospitality, so it is understandable that senior executives and board members don't have a detailed understanding of 'algo-bias' or what data their large language models were trained on.

Even if they are interested in subscribing to AI newsletters or following Reddit threads about quantum computing, most emerging technology news is written by tech people, for tech people, so with developments moving so quickly, it's a reasonable assumption that senior leaders are not always able to see the wood for the trees.

Most companies develop (and try to work to) three-, five- or seven-year strategic plans. These are easy to explain to employees and stakeholders. They're investor-friendly, banker-friendly, shareholder-friendly and – most commonly at five years – aligned with the average tenure of a chief executive, so offer a handy set of benchmarks to show whether he or she is doing a good job in running the firm.

A five-year plan underpins culture, values and priorities, and gives context to the most important elements of individual in-year plans, budgets, recruitment needs, annual objective setting and appraisal processes.

However, one of the things that marks out the old-world industrial and service businesses I have spent time with over the last year, is that they also tend to have a much longer-term plan in place, often 30, 50 or 100 years. This is usually much lighter touch, but helps to solidify a vision for how an organisation intends to continue existing many decades into the future.

Bear in mind that more than half (215) of the largest 400 businesses are already a century old, having been established before 1925. There are a number of reasons why these sorts of companies need to have a multi-generational strategic plan in place.

Firstly, geography: the size of these companies means that their factories, plants and facilities have often been in the same towns or cities for so many years that they become systemically important to local economies. Chief Executives with these infrastructural conditions will be very conscious of societal expectations on their company to have a plan in place, to continue energising the communities and ecosystems that have evolved around them over the years.

Secondly, there are career expectations among their workforce and talent pool: they are often organisations where several generations of the same families are likely to have worked in similar roles, so there is a cultural expectation that they will be able to guarantee positions for the next few generations of local talent, many of whom will choose to study relevant courses at schools or universities and may face familial pressure to join 'The Firm'.

Thirdly, in order to continue delivering on growth expectations, these organisations often need to lay down considerable capital investment on building factories and facilities, requiring the costs to be defrayed over a decade or more.

Finally, there is the issue of contractual stability. Companies who have been around forever are – rightly or wrongly – perceived to be a 'safe pair of hands' to institutional investors and governments, foreign and domestic. Not every product is a fast moving consumer good: there are plenty of companies currently fulfilling massive, multi-decade infrastructural or engineering contracts to build new cities, submarines, nuclear reactors, spaceships... Established conglomerates that look too big to fail, and have many years of experience and reputation in delivering consistently, will often win systemically important contracts over less experienced, more innovative players, even if they don't have the cheapest bid. Those institutional investors and governments are often prepared to pay a premium for a sense of assurance that these suppliers will still be around to finish and service the project in twenty or thirty years' time.

But here's the thing with a 100-year business plan: in the context of proper long-term thinking, technology really is a passing trend. When a corporate entity is projecting £40bn a year in revenues, spending £100m over three years on novel technologies represents little more than a rounding error on a balance sheet. One bank CFO I spoke to said that her CTO's £30m-a-year investment in AI was about the same size as the Exco's annual expenses budget. This made the spend easy to sign off, but also meant it wasn't viewed as strategically important.

'To get results in three or four years from machine learning, we need to spend now on the people and the technology. Because I can't promise results this year, the decision to invest in AI keeps being kicked into the long grass,' said a mining CIO in our interview. Several tech leaders reflected this view in the research, that senior executives in some companies are mostly concerned with quarter-to-quarter results, so big technology discussions are often deprioritised.

In a business that has already been around for 100 years, there will always be another technology that needs to be invested in, just like their predecessors brought in PCs or early automation. The inevitability of constantly having to invest in IT infrastructure lessens the sense of urgency and 100-year business plans are only helpful in this scenario when the people at the top are data-literate and have a long-term vision that sees tech as one of the keys to long-term competitiveness and resilience.

Embedding new technologies and ways of working in businesses with decades of established infrastructure can present a complex set of problems, not unlike decorating in in an old house: peeling off the wallpaper, only to find the walls are rotting underneath. The challenges of digital transformation can be particularly acute, for example, in manufacturing firms. Researchers at MIT Sloan found that 'Digital transformation for manufacturing differs substantially from transforming IT services or implementing e-commerce, because it requires combining the staged integration of physical assets with digital technologies. For these and other reasons, many manufacturers struggle to adopt transformative tech and end up misaligning and wasting their scarce specialised resources. As a consequence, their digital investments generally fail to enable the business transformation they seek.'[1]

The growing dependency on data

Executives and board members are rapidly becoming more dependent on data to make strategic decisions, though the research showed them to be lacking in data literacy and general understanding of data strategy.

Having surveyed 105 board members and senior executives (heads of, VPs, directors and C-suite) about interpreting management information, particularly with a view to understanding their Environmental, Societal and Governance (ESG) data and its relationship to their Net Zero corporate goals, it was clear that there is an urgent need to address the importance of learning to communicate in ways that senior leaders can understand.

Nearly nine in ten (87%) of respondents reported they felt that management information (MI) had become more complex over the previous three years, since the pandemic, while 70% said they had become more reliant on AI and data analytics over the same period.

Do you feel your management information (MI) has become more complex over the last three years?

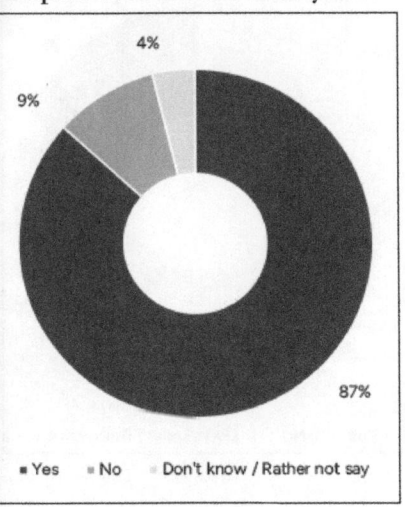

Have you become more reliant on data analytics / AI for your management information over the last three years?

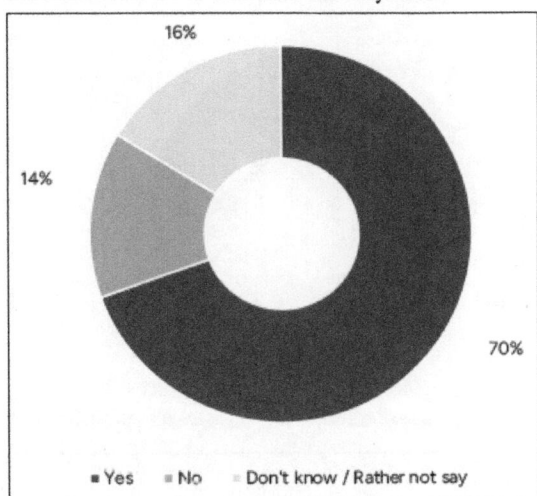

The research demonstrated that this dependency on data is only growing, as 78% of respondents reported that they expected to be 'largely' or 'completely' reliant on data to make business decisions moving forwards. However, this research flagged up that trust in data is becoming a significant issue for senior executives and board members.

When asked 'Do you feel that your executive team and board fully understand and trust the data they use to make strategic decisions with?', the answer was a stark and resounding 'no'. Bearing in mind that this survey was completed by a majority of people who self-identified as CEOs, board members and members of senior executive teams (and therefore were responding on behalf of themselves and their peers), only 23% of respondents said 'yes', while more than half (52%) said 'no' and a quarter (25%) said they didn't know or would rather not say.

This overwhelming vote of no confidence in executive data literacy corroborates findings in other research studies, including:

In the next two years, how reliant do you think you will be on data to make decisions in your business?

Do you feel that your executive team and Board fully understand and trust the data they use to make strategic decisions with?

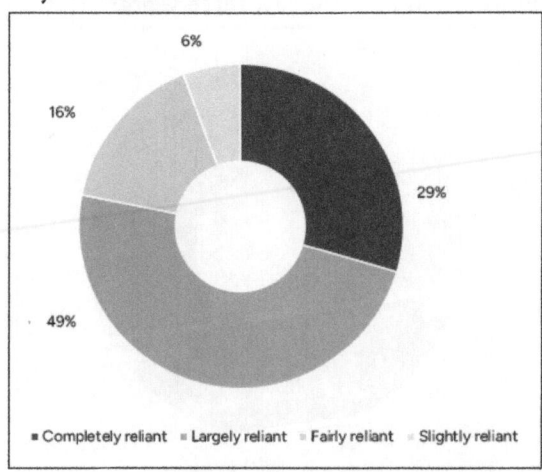

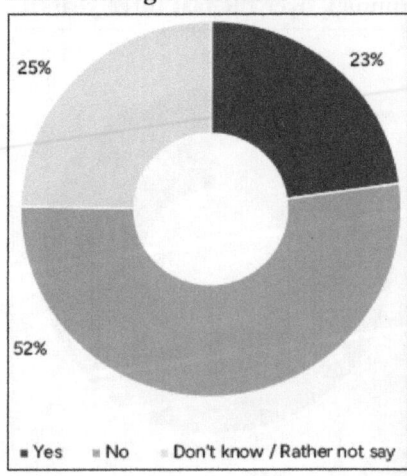

- Capgemini Research Institute (2022): 80% of business executives do not trust the data they receive to make decisions with;
- McKinsey & Company (2022): 47% of business leaders struggle to attract and reskill tech-savvy executive talent;
- Boston Consulting Group (2023): Leader engagement in transformation projects has dropped by 40% since the pandemic;
- Alix Partners (2022): 83% of CEOs say their board of directors impedes the process of adopting essential new technology solutions;
- And my own finding (covered in the next chapter) that the majority of CTOs, CIOs and technology leaders (58%) cited 'executive data literacy' as one of their top three risks to successful digital transformation.

I have seen one early sign that the tide may be beginning to turn: KPMG's 2023 *Global Tech Report* found boards and senior leaders starting to invest more freely in emerging technology: 38% of respondents said they now had buy-in from senior leaders for the deployment of emerging tools and technologies, a figure which increased from just 10% in the previous year's survey. The report also noted that the number was higher in the industrial manufacturing sector, where the figure had risen to 50%, with energy (44%), government (44%) and healthcare (43%) following not far behind.

However, whether this lone signal of increased executive buy-in is the sign of improving data literacy at senior levels or just that more boards signed off on investments in ChatGPT and other generative AI programmes in the twelve months between KPMG's annual technology reports, it is impossible to say. Perhaps not, as the same report also stated that nine out of ten digital leaders said they still needed to get better at helping the board to understand the potential of new technologies.

As an experienced board member and advisor, I can tell you that context is everything. It may help to understand some of the lenses through which senior executives and board members see the importance of data: reputation and risk, sustainability, supply chains, dark data, workforce efficiency, financial forecasting and capital investment.

Financial forecasting & capital investment

Probably the most frequent representation of 'data' for boards, CEOs and Excos is financial modelling, forecasting and planning data. No one gets to the top of a business like this without learning to find their way around a spreadsheet: board papers are always full of EBITDA financial projections, detailed analyses of capital investment plans and salary figures.

The downside is that executive leaders who can navigate their way around these numbers may not realise they suffer from low data literacy (after all, this is data!), yet they use it to make strategic decisions. A risk-averse CEO will prefer to table discussions with the board when he or she is fairly certain of the outcome of those discussions. For this reason, financial reporting at that level tends to be simple enough to cater for the lowest common denominator of knowledge around the table and curated to only show the data that is necessary to reach the desired outcome, with the minimum of critical challenge.

Workforce efficiency

One of the great promises of data-driven technologies is that they will offer magical solutions to age-old problems: 'Will we make more money?', 'Will we onboard more customers?', 'Will we gain an increased market share?', and the biggie... 'Will we be able to save money on headcount?' Large investments in tech are usually driven by the promise of making or saving money in the longer term. Reducing headcount (usually the biggest line of expenditure in a company's balance sheet) or enabling the same number of people to build more product in less time are both seen as desirable to shareholders, so announcements about using AI to achieve either of these goals tend to be share-price affecting.

Reputation & risk

A challenge shared by many of the old-world firms I have spoken to involves running safety-critical operations with heritage brands and legacy infrastructure. Leaders in these organisations are usually responsible for shareholder value and the livelihoods of tens of thousands of people.

Putting your very valuable eggs into a shiny new emerging technology basket is not at the top of many people's to-do list – especially with so many regulatory concerns and a media landscape more inclined to doom-mongering over the prospect of security breaches and AI 'hallucinations' (where generative AI provides well-reasoned misinformation).

It is important to note at this point the critical difference between customer-facing generative AI products and the way the most valuable industrial machine learning applications are deployed in large organisations. The rapid release of so many Large Language Model (LLM) products over the last few years has given rise to countless media stories about the dangers of AI – with examples where the bots have falsified information – but this generally isn't the case when looking at industrial ML, which is far less generalised and tends to focus on fixing a single problem, often trained on a very specific data set for the task at hand.

But even these closed-data AIs carry reputational risks, as it is usually impossible to develop greater diversity and representation around the data streams that make decisions for these systems when they are only working with limited data sets.

Explaining the difference in risk – or the scale of the opportunity – to a Chief Risk Officer with no technology experience is always going to be a challenge, when they don't have the vocabulary of data culture or an understanding of data strategy. As we'll explore in the next chapter, executive data literacy is rated by 58% of CTOs as being one of the top three risks to a successful data transformation, so upskilling those decision-makers is a high priority, which also creates its own risk around the capability of senior leaders to make competent decisions when it comes to using data.

A lack of data literacy at executive levels can breed uncertainty, which can be easily stoked if the person at the management table who is responsible for corporate reputation doesn't fully understand what is being proposed. If you want to understand why these people are the blockers to your great idea, answer yourself the following question: 'If this goes wrong, what will the front page of the *Daily Mail* say about it?' That's the question that keeps those people up at night.

Sustainability

The UK government's report *Our Waste, Our Resources: A Strategy for England* says:[2] 'Evidence suggests that 80% of the damage done to the environment from waste products can be avoided if more thoughtful decisions – about their design, the choice of materials and chemicals used, and how they will be distributed and sold to consumers – are made at the production stage.'

CEOs, CTOs and CIOs in major industrial firms are at an essential inflection point in history thanks to pressure from activists, investors, the media, their workforces and society at large, when it comes to sustainability. The decisions these people make in this moment will have an impact for generations.

The *Guardian* reported in 2024 that just 57 companies can be directly linked to 80% of the world's fossil fuel CO_2 emissions since the Paris Climate Accord in 2015, having previously said that just 100 firms in the world create the products – that get used by their customers and their customers' customers – which generate more than 71% of the world's carbon emissions.[3]

Many major companies have made commitments to reach Net Zero by 2050 and climate change is on every board agenda, conference agenda and political agenda. However, in 2022, Accenture found that only 26% of firms have the right data to underpin their ESG key performance indicators (KPIs) and that just 7% of companies have fully integrated their business, technology and sustainability strategies.

In many cases, these are the companies responsible for the majority of the planet's carbon emissions and they are actively working to reduce their impact on the environment, largely through digital transformation. After all, they recognise they are unlikely to get there without better use of the data at their disposal.

A lot of the firms making physical things at-scale expose the workers in their own businesses and in their supply chains to a much higher degree of risk of injury or even death from chemicals, high risk procedures, poor working environments, or badly designed manufacturing processes than those businesses which deal in services or digital-only products.

Caroline Gorski, former CEO of R² Factory at Rolls-Royce, put it most eloquently, saying 'The organisations that make and operate complex physical products across long life cycles are actively trying to upend the cost dynamics of operating those services and maintaining them by using data and artificial intelligence to better predict, control and manage them. However, by doing so, they may replace decades of human intelligence and risk management by using data to make decisions with increasing precision, employing machine intelligence that is powerful, but still immature.'

Companies like these understand they won't get to Net Zero without the application of machine learning and artificial intelligence, but they are learning that to get there, they will also need to be able to build out the flexibility, the agility and the responsiveness of the consumption networks and the power generating networks they depend on.

Several companies I have spoken to are using AI and machine learning to reduce waste consumption and optimise for the best choices about the raw materials that they use, how they combine them to make new products and then how they de-combine them at the end of their life cycles, in order to feed them back into a circular system.

However, a report called *Network Thinking* showed that only 10% of business leaders are confident their products are recycled or re-purposed at the end of their useful life, while a third have no knowledge of the circularity of their products at all.[4]

That research, conducted in December 2022, found that just under a third of business leaders felt they had some visibility over their company's Scope 3 emissions, but this figure rose to more than half in businesses where understanding their supply chain was rated as essential to meeting their ESG or Net Zero ambitions. ESG in supply chains was a major issue: only 19% of respondents overall expressed any confidence in the environmental and social impacts of their indirect suppliers.

For major industrial firms – especially when looking at how to unlock value from data – it is impossible to separate the sustainability issue from supply chains.

Supply chains

Since 2020, external factors influencing the resilience of industrial supply systems have included conflict, pandemic, recession, inflation, skills shortages, furlough schemes, lockdowns, isolationist trade policies, financial market uncertainty, regulatory change and Brexit.

Meanwhile, CTOs and CIOs in major industrial organisations, having spent much of the previous decade investing in and battling with their own digital transformation journeys, suddenly needed to pivot their priorities, with funding frozen, reduced or redirected away from innovation development activities and towards shoring up business-critical IT infrastructure, in order to cope with a series of 'unprecedented' market shocks.

For more than 25 years, the Federal Reserve Bank of New York's Global Supply Chain Pressure Index (GSCPI)[5] has tracked the state of global supply chains using data from the transportation and manufacturing sectors across seven economies. After falling quickly back to pre-pandemic levels after the initial shock of the first lockdowns in the second quarter of 2020, by December 2021, the GSCPI had hit an all-time high of 4.30, showing that global supply chain disruption had increased to eight times the average levels since records began. Meanwhile, after several years of rapid growth in adopting emerging technologies, investment plateaued when the pandemic began and only began to increase again in the latter half of 2023.

It is impossible to explain the functioning of the global economy – or indeed any modern economy – without explaining the idea of a supply chain. The image of a 'chain' seems to have been first suggested around the start of the 20th century, although it obviously describes something much older. Economies have long imported goods from outside their borders, just as they have long sought to export them there.

The problem with the image of a supply chain is that it can be highly misleading. A chain is a series of linear links. It would be more accurate to view modern supply chains as complex networks of interdependencies. The core links in the chain are dependent on each other, but also dependent on inputs or supporting frameworks of their own. No node on a supply chain can be viewed purely in isolation.

Failure, when it happens, can in practice emerge from any part of this network, and failures in any part can easily ripple through wider supply systems in unanticipated ways. Applying ideas like sustainability or risk to a supply chain, without considering the networks of which that chain is a part, jeopardises understanding much of what actually makes a supply model sustainable, or risky.

The strain on international supply chains through the pandemic, and subsequent global conflicts, have demonstrated their resilience as well as some of their weaknesses. Although this may prompt some simplification in supply systems, global sourcing will remain a fundamentally complex proposition, in which better use of data will be an integral part. Scrutiny of global sourcing choices is evolving in important ways, as are accountability frameworks for supply system managers.

Generally speaking, most industrial supply systems are relatively complex. In many complicated manufacturing supply systems, executives are dealing with the need to source very rare elements and raw materials. They may only have one or two suppliers in the world who can mine or make the components they need to be able to create whatever it is that they're producing. However, recent events have shown us that an ecological, biological or geopolitical disaster can decimate these single points of failure and disrupt entire supply networks in a very short space of time.

When trying to make manufacturing, logistics or buying decisions, human brains are limited to optimising for obvious metrics like cost or supply quantity, so industrial companies have invested heavily in developing ML optimisation engines to simultaneously account for variables including route optimisation, supply security, geography, carbon cost and weather-related uncertainty.

A complex mapping exercise of direct suppliers, and suppliers to suppliers, of a firm is generally impractical, if not impossible. Supply system partners may have different levels of data collection or management sophistication, which is why it is becoming increasingly important for businesses to collaborate with their up- and down-stream supply partners, in order to build practical solutions to capture second-order risks, interlinkages and dependencies across the network.

With such increasing complexity, many large organisations are leveraging AI, machine learning and data analytics to better understand the risks and sustainability of their choices, trying to ensure that by fixing a problem in one node of their interconnected supply system, they don't inadvertently cause other, bigger problems to surface in different places.

The emergence of 'dark data'

Whether discussing supply chain issues, risks or sustainability, many of the technology leaders (if not yet the operational leaders) I spoke to shared their concerns over the growing importance of 'dark data'.

A relatively new concept, various estimates suggest that between 80% and 95% of all data produced doesn't adhere to a predefined data model or schema, making it unstructured, or 'dark'. There is a widespread suspicion that hidden within this sea of unmanaged and untapped data lies incredible transformational value.

The implication is that while structured data can show you what is happening, only unstructured data will tell you why. The 2022 *Digital Leadership Report*[6] from Nash Squared suggested that firms are struggling to realise value from data, finding that although 64% of CTOs and CIOs thought data analytics could deliver competitive advantage, only 21% felt they were effective at using data insights to drive value in their businesses. Meanwhile, the 2022 *Cloud Security Report*[7] from Networx, which said that 80% of businesses store sensitive data in the cloud, also found that 79% of organisations reported 'moderate' to 'high' levels of concern around proliferation of dark data but were unsure how to approach the issue. Also in 2022, research firm Absolute Market Insights[8] suggested that the global dark analytics market was ripe for rapid growth, with a 2021 value of $789.3m in 2021 forecast to increase at a compound annual growth rate of 25.8% by 2030.

To quote a Chief Digital Officer I interviewed from a pharmaceutical firm, 'Data and AI are important to businesses in two ways. First, they help us to make better decisions. And second, they can make the invisible visible.'

This is why recognising the importance of dark data is emerging as an area of real concern to leaders of industrial businesses. Global supply chains are data-driven entities. Each node in a supply network generates exponential volumes of data at high velocity that companies are often unable to keep up with, resulting in vast amounts of dark data being collected but not understood.

Consequently, when companies are navigating complexity in supply systems, they are doing so from an inherently limited position. When asked, more than four in five CEOs, CTOs and CIOs felt it was likely that solutions to their supply system complexity were hidden in the 'dark data' their business collects but doesn't analyse effectively.

Optimisation at scale is relevant for every major industrial organisation, so by combining AI tools like computer vision, natural language processing and advanced analytics, it may be possible to uncover previously inaccessible dark data. So if leaders could access – and critically, understand – more data, to extract meaningful information to help them manage their supply systems, they would be better positioned to adjust quickly to sudden shifts in demand, keep up with regulatory reporting requirements such as emissions monitoring and management, and overall have a more sophisticated view of their supply networks.

With the right technology and expertise, dark data can be harnessed to help companies navigate complexity and maximise the potential of network thinking. However, to effectively mine and interpret the immense volumes of dark data, companies don't just need access to advanced digital tools... they need to understand the right questions to ask and the right data sources to interrogate, in order to extract meaningful insights that can really make an impact.

3

Culture: why humans reject transformation

So much of being able to push through digital innovation in any working environment depends on our ability to understand and communicate the value of data more fluently, so that sceptics can be converted into champions. This is no great surprise, when the majority of leaders feel their own businesses lack a basic level of technological competence: the KPMG *Global Tech Report* in 2024 found that 57% of organisations reported that flaws in their foundational enterprise IT systems disrupted business-as-usual on a weekly basis, so the necessary baseline of trust in tech's ability to make things better is already low in many cases.

Anyone who has ever tried to innovate in a corporate environment will have encountered resistance from other people who will either be impacted by change or perceive that they could be. This chapter explores how humans adapt (or fail to adapt) to change and how you can help them to overcome their objections.

Many of their business concerns are very real, so we can learn a lot from trying to understand their perspectives. As one General Counsel of a global bank, who sits on the Exco and is also secretariat to the board, put it in an interview: 'The budget challenge in digital transformation is not trivial. The way I like to think about it is to harvest budget efficiency and then use that to invest in new capabilities, focused on effectiveness.'

The gap in communication between those who can make big strategic decisions and those who want to drive change in their organisations is often a giant chasm, and it is the innovator's job to find ways to communicate which close the space, rather than widen it.

Transformation isn't cheap and isn't easy, so – even when budget can be released – the final decision often sits with the executive team or board. Which may be why the most frequently cited, shared and discussed piece of insight from the digital transformation research I carried out in June 2023 is what I went on to call the CTO Risk Register. I asked senior technology professionals to look at transformation through the lens of a corporate risk register and to consider the common reasons for failure as obstacles that could be mitigated.

The results were incredibly instructive: CTOs, CIOs and technology leaders said that over two thirds (69%) of the biggest risks to successful digital transformation were cultural issues:

1. Poor data literacy at executive level
2. Lack of workplace digital culture
3. Limited ability to hire specialist tech talent
4. Low investment in continuous digital education
5. Low enterprise-wide trust in data

The remaining 31% of the risks cited involved strategic and operational issues, such as 'poor data quality', 'poor data strategy' and 'data is siloed/difficult to access', as outlined on the following page.

As the CTO at a global electronics firm said in one of the subsequent round tables, 'It's great having a big tech strategy. But employers are struggling to find the people to execute their plans.'

Interestingly, 58% of our respondents cited 'poor executive data literacy' as one of their top three risks to successful transformation.

From this list, please rank your top three concerns on your digital transformation risk register

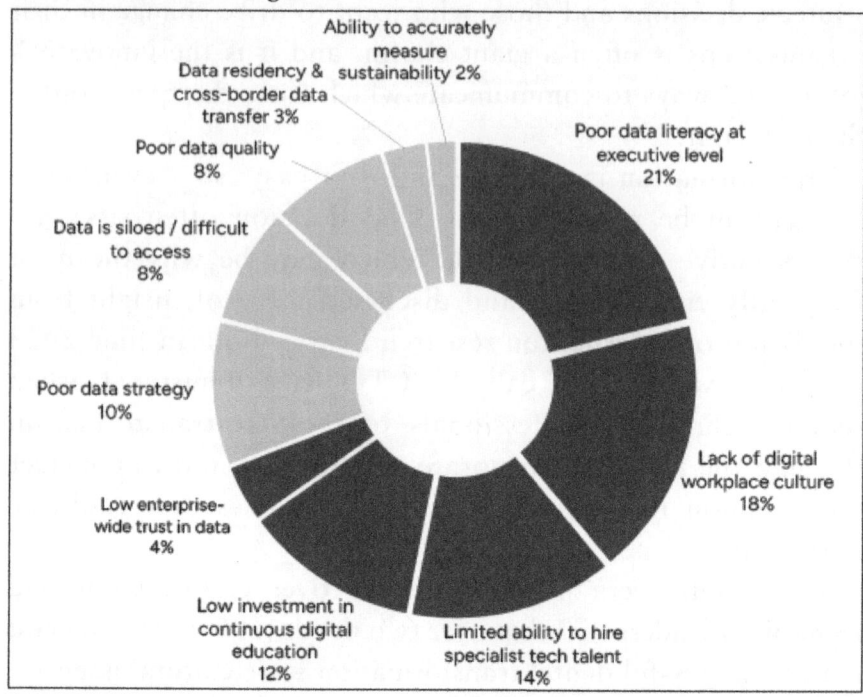

So, what is the problem here? Why don't more senior executives have an innate understanding of data and what it means? The example I cite in data literacy workshops refers to a type of data set which is publicly available to anyone of any age with a television, radio, laptop or mobile phone: the application of science and technology to predict the atmospheric conditions for a particular time and location (also known as the weather forecast).

While everyone has access to the same data when watching a weather forecaster on the telly predict a 30% chance of rain, humans have an uncanny ability to believe different things about the data. According to the Royal Meteorological Society, 'Some people have interpreted it to mean that it will rain 30% of the time, others that it will affect 30% of the area.' Others may take it to mean that it will rain at 30% of full volume (as if 100% would be 'complete' rain and 10% only 'slight' rain). Of course, what the forecaster is saying is that on previous days which have had similar atmospheric conditions to today, it ended up raining on 30% of those days. Therefore, there is a 30% statistical likelihood that there will be some rain today.

When I provide this example, there is usually a ripple of awkward laughter around the room: some people think others must be stupid for misinterpreting something so simple as a weather forecast, others feel embarrassed that their long-held assumptions have just been challenged. Then I tell them I'm one of the stupid ones. I have more than a passing understanding of what data is and how it is analysed – I help businesses with their data strategies, for goodness' sake! I know exactly how weather forecasts are modelled and if I think about it for a moment, I know what 30% chance of rain means... except that I cannot escape my own belief, innately held since childhood, which is that it will rain 30% of the time!

The remaining significant issues in the CTO Risk Register were around data, the biggest being 'Poor data strategy', which is not unrelated to the cultural risks. With quality and accessibility polling at 8% each, data residency (challenges around the geographical location of where data is collected and stored) and the ability to use data to accurately measure sustainability also featured.

The chart clearly demonstrates – in a way that even the least tech-savvy board director could understand – that the majority of obstacles to digital transformation concern the humans, not the technology. This issue was widely recognised in all of the group discussions and often mentioned in my interviews with both technical and operational business leaders.

Why does everybody hate data?

People generally don't like what they don't understand. Nicholas Carleton, a psychology professor at the University of Regina, Canada, believes the 'unknown' represents one of humanity's 'fundamental fears'.[1] 'In most cases, uncertainty appears to be a core element of anxiety,' he says. 'Uncertainty can intensify how threatening a situation feels,' agrees Boston Consulting Group psychologist Ema Tanovic.

So what is data? As consumers, we understand data to be something personal to us. It's been said that GDPR legislation ended up being the biggest crowdsourced PR campaign in history. Every business in Europe suddenly began begging consumers to opt back in, or risk losing out on discounts or personal offers. It is unclear how many people were even aware of what personal data was or how it was used before May 2018, but now every internet user needs to consider it whenever they open a website and decline cookies, or whenever they receive an email they didn't specifically request.

Consequently, most of us understand 'data' to be our contact details, perhaps our location, sometimes our biometric information. A common view is that we usually have to trade something personal, in order to get something free, with a reasonable expectation that Silicon Valley startups will sell what they have to the highest bidder in return for us being able to use a smartphone app that makes our lives easier.

But for businesses, 'What is data?' is a much more complex question, which varies as much by a person's occupation as it does by the sector their company operates in.

Most people working in office jobs recognise data as the content of spreadsheets, databases and CRM systems. Marketing professionals might see data as something to be segmented, analysed and targeted, looking for particular demographics or socioeconomic groups, in order to pitch an advertising campaign or mailshot. If you work in HR, your principal understanding of data might be around payroll or reward information, the security of your employees' details, or a way to calculate the diversity of your recruitment pool. In a finance team, it could be the balance sheet, the integrity of your investor pack, or how you represent various metrics for your board.

Then, depending on which industry you're in, you may find data is essential to mapping the carbon emissions in your downward supply chain; or finding efficiencies in the way you manufacture products; or how you design a piece of machinery so it is 10% more effective; or how you reposition point-of-sale items to increase revenue; or how you identify fraud, or vulnerable customers, from call-centre interactions; or it could tell you how fast your buildings, vehicles or equipment are depreciating; or how you look out for suspicious activity that might warn of cyber-attacks...

'Data' means different things to different people and it impacts almost every job, from the shop assistant taking a contactless payment to the nurse scanning a patient's wristband before giving out medication, to the CEO trying to make sense of their employees' net promoter scores.

And that's just the obvious stuff, when your data mostly consists of words and numbers. One of the struggles many old-world industrial firms face when it comes to trying to get value from artificial intelligence and machine learning is that a lot of their intellectual property (IP) is hidden away in different forms: floorplans, hand-drawn schematics, physical prototypes, chemical formulae, images, scientific notation.

Most of these are not in machine-readable formats, but they are all types of data. As one engineering CTO told me, 'A significant amount of our IP is hidden in schematics, drawings, spreadsheets and local computers. In a 30,000-person business, only a handful of people realise that this is data. It's data that isn't known or machine-readable or searchable, some of it is literally on paper.'

Besides which, data-driven technologies move so fast it often feels that as soon as you catch up with one long enough to get your head around a new piece of software, it's rushed off into the distance and been replaced with another.

So, people don't like problems they can't solve. And if you can't clearly or consistently define a problem, how can you solve it? Over the course of my workshops with senior technical and operational executives from many leading organisations trying to tackle digital transformation, I have developed a schema – detailed in Part Three – to help identify the best ways to remove the fear and lean in to the powerful possibilities that data can offer.

So, what do people need to feel safe?

In the next section, we will explore the various cultural blockers that occur naturally across all sorts of working environments, each of which can negatively impact worker morale, hope, ambition and psychological safety (later in the book, we'll look at how to solve for them). Each of these blockers makes successful transformation harder. But first, it's worth taking a quick contextual refresher on some of the cognitive and behavioural theories that underpin what your employees may need, in order to envisage themselves succeeding.

1. **Maslow's Hierarchy of Needs**
   Arguably the most famous triangle diagram in business school lore, American psychologist Abraham Maslow theorised that basic human needs must be met before people can reach their full potential. He created a 'hierarchy of needs' that breaks down what those needs look like, in order:

   - Basic physiological needs: food, water and shelter;
   - Safety needs: health, financial security and physical safety;
   - Social needs: a sense of belonging, community and what we now call inclusion;
   - Esteem needs: respect, recognition, being valued;
   - Self-actualisation needs: personal growth and developing one's full potential.

2. **Parsons' Trait and Factor Theory**
   American social reformer and academic Frank Parsons laid the foundation for what is often considered to be the traditional career development approach. In his view, career

development could be broken down into three steps, based on matching people to opportunities:

- People's patterns of traits can be used to create individual profiles;
- Occupational profiles can identify factors for success in available jobs;
- Individual profiles can then be matched with the occupational profiles.

3. Super's Developmental Self-Concept Theory

Donald Super built on Parsons' work, by suggesting that career development should be an unfolding process, not a point-in-time decision, in which (a) career development could be seen as a lifelong process with a series of developmental stages, and (b) career selection is not a one-shot decision but the cumulative outcome of a series of decisions.

Super proposed five stages, based roughly on developmental age, that reflect a person's maturity and readiness to make career choices:

- **Growth** (age 4–13), developing capacities, attitudes, preferences and forming a general understanding of the world of work;
- **Exploration** (age 14–24), identifying interests and capabilities and working out how to fit in with various occupations;
- **Establishment** (age 25–44), securing initial positions and pursuing chances for further advancement;
- **Maintenance** (45–65), holding on, keeping up, and innovating to remain relevant;
- **Disengagement** (over 65), deceleration, retirement planning, and retirement living.

4. Holland's Theory of Vocational Types

John Holland believed that people who had jobs that matched their personalities were much happier and more fulfilled than those who did not. His theory suggests that people project their views of self and workplace onto occupational types and make career decisions that satisfy their preferred personal orientations.

Holland created the RIASEC model which identifies six modal types and occupational environments they might be a good match for:

- **Realistic**: interested in activities requiring motor coordination and physical work tasks, such as mechanic, engineer, farmer;
- **Investigative**: motivated by organising and understanding, rather than dominating or persuading, such as technologist, scientist, geologist;
- **Artistic**: attracted to physical, expressive activities, but tending to dislike structure and rigidity, such as musician, actor, designer;
- **Social**: leaning towards social interaction and helping others, not interested in isolative activities, such as teacher, psychologist, caseworker;
- **Enterprising**: aspiration to attain power and status and enjoyment of persuading others, such as salesperson, media personality, business executive;
- **Conventional**: preferring rules, structures and regulations, such as accountant, banker, court reporter.

5. Bandura's Social Cognitive Theory

Canadian-American psychologist Albert Bandura theorised that learning occurs within a social context and that behaviour results from the interaction between personal factors, environmental influences and behavioural patterns. He believed that if behaviour is rewarded (with positive reinforcement), we are likely to imitate it; however, if behaviour is punished, imitation is less likely. He suggested that this 'social learning theory' could be used to explain:

- How basic interests develop;
- How choices are made;
- How success is achieved.

Physician, heal thyself: what have you learned?

For anyone trying to drive a transformation programme, it is critical to recognise the importance of 'meeting people where they are' in their own development: everybody will be at a different point in their personal and professional journeys and will have a variety of skills, competencies and experiences to bring to the table. Equally, I recommend you work out where you are on your own journey.

As a leadership coach, there is a fascinating exercise I sometimes carry out with my clients, called 'What I have learned?' I ask them to reflect on the last few jobs they have had and ask themselves the following five simple questions about each one:

- What did you love about the role/company?
- What did you hate about the role/company?
- What was your proudest achievement in the job?
- What did you learn about how businesses operate?
- What did you learn about the way you work with others?

I recommend trying it. It only takes a few minutes and it's an excellent way to distil your career down into a handful of really key life lessons and can be helpful in identifying what matters to you and the next steps you want to take.

I mention this here, because when I tried it myself (before inflicting it on others), I experienced quite a profound revelation relating to the experiences that had shaped me in the companies I had worked in. As someone who has often been hired or promoted because I'm 'that guy' who thinks outside the box, takes risks and enthuses others with a passion for trying new things, I have come up against a lot of institutional resistance to change during my career.

Here are five things I learned about the way businesses operate:

- People do business with people they like (or identify with);
- Great leadership is energising, poor leadership is exhausting – it takes much more work to conceal weakness than it does to celebrate strength;
- Senior executives are just as scared of getting things wrong as junior employees, but they suffer from a greater degree of 'imposter syndrome';
- Size matters: appetite for risk is inextricably linked to the scale of a leader's accountability (to owners, shareholders or stakeholders);
- The potential for failure is a bigger motivator to make decisions than the potential for success.

Try it for yourself. What have you learned in your career to date? And how can you put this knowledge to good use in your change programme?

What are the cultural blockers?

When I consider the journey of digital transformation, I'm reminded of my oldest friend, who recently had a kidney transplant. It isn't an outpatient procedure: it is a long, complicated operation that requires weeks of preparation and months of recuperation. Long-term success of the operation depends on a huge number of variables – the fitness of the new kidney, the resilience of his body, the way his other organs react, the skill of the surgeons, the quality of the aftercare, the regime of pharmaceuticals required, the way those drugs interact with his body chemistry... and even if they get everything 'right', there is still a considerable risk of tissue rejection (the host body recognising that the new kidney is alien) for up to 18 months after the surgery.

At time of writing, he is still receiving a great deal of follow-up care, with further invasive procedures, but thankfully, his prognosis is very good. But if any of those variables had been managed differently, the transplant might have failed. One of the biggest variables is the anti-rejection medication, which is toxic to the human body and needs to managed very carefully, as every patient is different. If the levels are too low, the tissue will reject and the kidney will fail; too high and the toxicity of the drug will damage the kidney and other organs.

This is an extreme analogy, but one that feels very personal and relevant to me. Digital transformation is not as simple as swapping out one way of working for another and just expecting it to 'take'. The people working in your organisation are the host body – after all, what is a company without its people? – and transformation is a process which needs to be managed and monitored carefully, to avoid the corporate equivalent of 'tissue rejection'.

Drawing on my research and the work of academics, management consultancies and organisational psychologists, and by working with a group of experienced technical and domain experts, it has been possible to identify 11 mindset and 15 behavioural blockers, which this book will tell you how to fix.

Part Three lists positive solutions and practical actions that anyone who wants to succeed at digital transformation can take. But first of all, we need to understand the problem space...

Mindset

1. Fear of the Unknown

One of the long-term effects of the pandemic is that many more people than ever before suffer from increased anxiety around change and uncertainty. This fear can play out in interesting ways in work environments, where employees often feel they have less control than in their personal lives.

Bringing in new processes, expectations, hierarchy or technology can change the dynamics of people's ways of working and signs of resistance can include: (a) bringing up reasons that something cannot be done – 'but we've always done it this way'; (b) agreeing to a stated objective or commitment, then finding (seemingly unrelated) reasons not to deliver on it later; (c) procrastinating and putting off doing things the new way 'because this is urgent and I need to get it right this time – I'll try the new way next time'; (d) finding holes in an argument in order to avoid or delay taking action.

2. Rigidity

When people care about what they do, they will care about the quality of their work. In their own way, they may have spent years honing a particular process within the bounds of their job remit so it is easier for them and/or better for the customers or stakeholders. By the time you come along with all your high-falutin' change aspirations, they may be particularly resistant to 'improving' a process or way of working they already consider to be the best it can be.

They are likely to be rigid in their approach, not open to innovation in something they feel is close to perfect. They may take your aspiration to improve to be a criticism of their work. This defensiveness is especially common in hierarchical environments, where people may not feel they have a lot of 'wriggle room' to make their own improvements and may experience the idea of transformation as further disempowering them.

3. Low empathy

Everyone I have ever met has had a terrible line manager at some point in their career. Since the publication of Jon Ronson's *The Psychopath Test*,[2] much has been written about the propensity (with estimates anywhere between

4–12%) of people with psychopathic traits to become CEOs and senior leaders. Academic Karen Landay, who has studied this trend, reports that people with psychopathic tendencies are slightly more likely to become bosses. 'They are typically very charming on the surface, they are bold and not afraid,' she says, 'they don't care that they are hurting you. They will do what they have to do.'

As the research in Chapter One showed, 'leading with empathy and kindness' is rated by technology leaders to be the most important indicator for a successful digital transformation programme, but sadly many bosses are found lacking in the empathy or humility stakes and employees tend to 'follow the leader' when it comes to exhibiting behaviours. Environments where emotional intelligence (EQ) isn't valued tend to be far more resistant to innovation and change.

4. **Lack of entrepreneurship**
   The majority of old-world businesses that this research focused on prize predictability and consistency over innovation and entrepreneurship. This can be for very good reasons but does tend to inhibit 'out-of-the-box' thinking and is one of the variables that need to be monitored closely in any transformation programme. If entrepreneurship is disincentivised by company culture, it may feel like the least safe option, so employees are more likely to keep brilliant new ideas and approaches to themselves.

5. **Linear thinking**
   Linear thinking is the traditional mode of ideation that businesses commonly deploy for problem-solving by using logic, past data and existing solutions. It is how leaders make sense of a changing environment, but it is limited by its scope and logic. Not having permission to consider problems from new angles or using alternative sources of information can inhibit a necessary mindset shift in some working cultures.

6. The pale, male and stale conundrum

While there has been a lot of progress in the last few years on DE&I, many leaders don't realise that organisations with diverse management teams have 19% higher revenues due to innovation,[3] or that 67% of job seekers consider a diverse workforce an important factor when evaluating companies to apply to,[4] or that companies in the top quartile for gender diversity on their executive team were 21% more likely to experience above-average profitability.[5]

The UK's *FTSE Women Leaders* report in February 2023 found that women held 40% of board roles and 27% of executive committee jobs in FTSE350 companies.[6] Nineteen boards reported either one or no women on the board and 77 firms in the sample had not only failed to make progress, but gone backwards since the 2021 report.

Meanwhile, the Parker Review found in 2022 that ethnic minority directors accounted for 11% of all FTSE 250 board positions, mostly non-executive directors (NEDs).[7] External scrutiny and voluntary target setting are achieving results in changing the way boards and senior management teams look, but for many of these organisations, there is still some way to go before diversity of thought and approach filters through to the way they operate.

Women on Boards showed in its 2024 report *The Hidden Truth* that gender representation in the UK boardroom had progressed significantly over the past decade, due to a collective focus on a business-led approach to driving change.[8]

However, the report cautioned that more work is needed to reach gender parity in the 'four key roles': the most influential positions in the boardroom – Chair, Senior Independent Director (SID), Finance Director (FD) and Chief Executive. Currently only 13% of these roles are held by women, while just 5.7% are held by women of colour. While all-male boards appear to be a thing of the past in enterprise firms, ensuring that all women are part of the progress made is vital. With just ten female CEOs in FTSE 250 companies and only 25 women of colour appointed across 3,452 'key roles', this may not be the case.

7. Slowness to adapt

Many organisations have resistance to cultural change baked into their DNA and the people in them will instinctively add complication where there could be simplicity. These attitudes often reinforce structural barriers which prevent adoption of even the most basic principles of Agile and Lean working practices. Moving from protectionist views of work as the subject of labour to the object of customer-centricity is a challenging mindset-shift for many, as new ways of working and new technologies can bring with them a fear of obsolescence and redundancy.

8. Institutional thinking

The larger and older an organisation is, the more likely it is to have well-established practices and processes which eliminate variety in system design, customer experience or product quality. Predictability is seen as key to consistency of output, and so any new way of working which threatens the status quo might be viewed with suspicion, which can lead to poor adoption, which in turn will likely limit its impact. Witnessing poor returns from a mismanaged change programme will only reinforce that suspicion and reduce employees' risk appetite to try the next new thing that comes along.

9. Seriousness

'Work to live, don't live to work' is a common and perfectly reasonable mantra adopted by billions of people in a capitalist society. The office, plant, shop or factory is where we go to do serious things that we get paid for, so we can spend our weekends and holidays doing things we actually enjoy. It is understandable that most people take their work seriously.

I have been extremely lucky in my career, that in 2005 I discovered for the first time what it was like to wake up excited about going to work and, since then, that enthusiasm has always filtered through to the teams I have managed. The best bosses I've ever had have shared my view that work should be fun, that a workplace filled with laughter and bonhomie is one filled with ideas, where it is safe to experiment and take chances. In my experience, experimentation = fun, fun = productive, and productive = successful. Most large, hierarchical organisations have built-in, structural safeguards to prevent workers from using too much imagination, rather than creating safe spaces where experimentation can thrive.

10. Risk aversion

Fear of failure is so embedded in the upper echelons of large companies that executives and board directors often view most opportunities to change through the lens of risk: What could go wrong? Will I get fired if it fails? How will it affect the share price? How will it impact our staff? What new danger does it expose us to? What could be the unforeseen implications?

Aversion to risk is one of the single most common barriers to innovation in any established corporate entity. It is particularly prevalent in highly regulated sectors (finance, insurance, defence, pharmaceuticals), ones where missteps can negatively impact the safety or wellbeing of members of the public (civil engineering, aerospace, healthcare) and publicly traded entities (where decisions impact shareholder value, and thus the resilience of the company itself). Decision-makers in these environments are conditioned to weigh every change against the risk it carries. And that approach cascades down through the organisation.

11. Data illiteracy

Everyone's already busy doing their own job! Why do they have to learn about data as well? Data strategy is too often hampered by siloed concerns about IT systems and data usage, and too rarely an integral part of a comprehensive strategy. This has begun to change. As more companies appoint Chief Data Officers or move Chief Technology Officers to the top table, data strategy is beginning to align far more closely to the overall business strategy in those organisations.

However, in about half of the companies I spoke to, technology is still seen as one of many services provided from within the Chief Operating Officer's remit, while in some of the others, technology leaders who are on the Exco report that discussions about data are still frequently de-prioritised in boardrooms.

Each of these mindset barriers is an obstacle to creating a positive environment for transformation. Consequently, there is a higher prevalence of the following challenging behaviours, all of which can be addressed...

Behaviours

12. Role-limited training

Obviously the provision of adequate training for employees is a good thing, as is investment in role-specific training for people who want to gain deeper expertise in their specialisms. But this focus on educating members of your team to be better at their actual job can sometimes result in preventing them from developing broader skills and insights which could enable them to grow in unexpected ways.

My mother in-law always said that, 'A weed is just a flower you didn't plant yourself': if you don't have an environment where your people can explore new learning resources – perhaps in digital skills that may not seem immediately relevant to the role they have – they may never identify the passion that gets them up in the morning, or become the leader you never knew you they had the potential for, or come up with the business idea that could take your organisation to the next level. Don't forget the D in L&D!

13. Fostering unhealthy competition

Conflicts at the top of a business inevitably filter down and even if they are not actively instructed to, teams will 'follow the leader' by competing against each other, undermining – and even hindering – each other's successes. Although these are some of the most obvious traits of a toxic working environment, this 'us and them' battle-ready state is often encouraged by leaders, because it feels tribal, can enhance cohesion within teams and engender ferocious loyalty. However, it mostly achieves these things at the expense of productivity and causes missed opportunities by inhibiting cross-team collaboration.

14. Reinforcing silos

An environment where learning is limited to specific roles, and where teams compete against each other, is unlikely to benefit from a great deal of knowledge-sharing. Quite the opposite, in fact: in environments where knowledge = power, middle-managers often find themselves incentivised to protect what they know and keep it within the team to ensure continued competitive advantage. This becomes particularly challenging when building a data strategy, if several of your key stakeholders become protective about a single data source and won't reveal to anyone else what it is telling them.

15. Shutting down possibility

If people don't have a sense of psychological safety and don't get a sense of joy from their work, they are unlikely to explore new approaches, insights or viewpoints. Without that sense of possibility, who knows what opportunities your business is missing out on? When the incentive structure rewards fealty and compliance, why would anyone challenge their ideas of how things should or could be done? It's often more effort than it's worth.

16. Keeping ideas to yourself

In well-established power structures, often found in old-world hierarchical organisations, or just in businesses where leaders feel insecure, it is often possible to find 'divide-and-conquer' or 'command-and-control' strategies at work, ensuring that information is locked down and limiting the number of voices allowed to have opinions. In these environments, thinking outside of the box can feel like a dangerous game and innovators learn to remain silent, or leave for greener pastures.

17. Disempowering talent

There are two main reasons businesses want to improve diversity: those who want to change the way they are seen and those who want to change the way they act. Which one are you? Teams where difference of opinion is met with judgement or retribution are more likely to hire in their own image. Strong leaders welcome challenge and will hire people who have a variety of opinions, backgrounds and experiences (and make them feel welcome and valued). Weak leaders will often hire followers – the meeker the better – and may interpret constructive challenge as destructive threat.

18. Relying on 'gut instinct'

'This is the way we do things here.' 'We tried that before, it didn't work.' 'Nice idea, but the boss likes it done this way.'

Intuition is where the unconscious brain rifles through its stored knowledge of past experiences to find the most likely answer to our problems, without us consciously recalling the memories that power those feelings. While it has been millennia since humans have had to hide in a cave from a sabre-toothed tiger, it is the primitive threat measure in the brain that drives what we call 'gut instinct'. Most people, when asked, will tell you they have excellent instincts and trust them implicitly.

Relying on subjective, anecdotal or circumstantial evidence is often impossible to defend, but in companies where the most powerful voice is assumed to be the most important, it is easier to defer to someone else's gut instincts than to use data to make a decision.

19. Silencing dissent

A team which is not engaged or empowered will struggle to find a collective voice, will learn only to look to its leader for reasoning and will rarely feel safe enough to 'speak truth to power'. This lack of agency will compound toxicity in the work environment and will limit the personal and professional growth of all concerned.

That lack of agency can impact managers and the kinds of ideas they will allow in their teams. A research paper in *Organization Science* posits that, 'Low-status managers feel the need to be territorial – that is, to maintain and protect their existing work domains from potential infringement by others – and therefore refrain from endorsing their employees' novel, yet useful ideas.' [9]

20. Complaining, not fixing

If your team becomes entrenched in a silo and neglects to collaborate effectively with others, there is a real risk that they will be seen as 'Them' in other parts of the organisation. If they become overly dependent on a leader to tell them what to do, there will be no incentive to find solutions to their own problems. The things that make their jobs harder will soon become points of complaint, or demands for support, either passed up to their manager, or 'lobbed over the fence' to another team, which may handle the request with resentment.

21. Knowing it all

Success breeds superiority and if for whatever reason your team (and its leader) are smashing all their targets, this can give rise to an arrogance which plays out in a number of different ways. If you're already good at what you do, there is less incentive to improve. Without an aspiration to get better, there will likely be less willingness to collaborate, share or learn. Which makes you less responsive to change.

In their book *Transforming Organizations*, Michael Anderson and Miranda Jefferson refer to this need as 'critical reflection': 'The ability to perceive and analyse situations and then formulate wise responses to complex problems'.

So, congratulations on being the best team this quarter. But what happens next quarter, when the variables aren't in your favour? Who are you going to ask for help if you've shown you already know everything?

22. Negative disruption

If you try to bring in any kind of organisational transformation without humility, or being mindful of how people will react to change, you may find yourself up against any number of viable objections. If other humans in the business can't see why the change is positive, or are nervous about what this means for their jobs, or can't see how the disruption positively benefits the wider company objectives, they are likely to resist with every tool at their disposal.

Not considering how others may be adversely affected, or taking time to help them to understand the net-positive impact of the change on how they perform their roles, can shoot down a transformation programme before it has even left the ground.

23. Running away from danger

If your organisation hasn't brought people along on the journey towards transformation, and leaders haven't demonstrated empathy in disrupting everyone, then a minuscule risk appetite will be reinforced – in fact, it will become something of a self-fulfilling prophecy. If your people don't believe a change programme can succeed, I assure you it will not. If leaders are not prepared to show the courage of their convictions and lean in to a transformation, no one else will either.

24. Dying by 1,000 papercuts

Failing fast, learning through feedback and iterating are essential behaviours in successful change programmes. If an organisation has a low-risk appetite, it follows it will probably also have a low tolerance for failure. Given that up to 88% of all digital transformations fail, attempting one in an environment where failure is not an acceptable outcome increases the pressure on those responsible and decreases the likelihood that failure will be acknowledged early enough. This can mean those involved may feel like they are in a slow-motion car crash, which will negatively impact morale and increase feelings of powerlessness.

25. Ignoring feedback

Mistakes can be costly – in time, money and credibility – so it may feel to those involved in a slow-failing change that their reputations (and prospects) are being damaged by the process.

Symptoms of the low morale this causes can include not bothering to (a) document processes; (b) pay attention to feedback about why the failure occurred; or (c) review processes or feedback to identify improvement opportunities.

These failures all increase the likelihood that next time (if there is a next time) you won't be able to avoid repeating the same pitfalls and won't improve your chances of success.

26. Failing to iterate

Iteration is probably the most important word in the world of Lean and Agile. In my first book, back in 2017,[10] I included an observation on the way event managers can use the cycle of repetition with real-life delegates to improve processes and ways of working over three years: year one, they run a conference or dinner the way they think they are expected to; year two, they use the feedback to make fundamental improvements to how the event operates; year three, they use feedback again from those changes to make the event as perfect as they can.

Not all jobs offer such obvious, or cyclical, feedback loops, but there are lessons for us all in how to identify opportunities to build them in. Iterating effectively may feel difficult, but it is game-changing.

These 26 mindset and behavioural challenges have been developed with a group of leading technology and operational C-suite executives in enterprise firms. They represent the problem spaces that most large businesses face when tackling digital transformation.

But it isn't all bad news! There are simple ways to solve for each of these obstacles. The first 26 elements in the Periodic Table of Data Strategy Elements in Part Three – developed with the same group of experts – correspond with the numbering of the mindset and behavioural challenges listed above, for ease of reference.

The more of these you can solve for – and the solutions are practical and relatively easy to implement – the greater the chance that your change programme will be successful.

PART TWO

Why industrial AI is destined to fail

4

AI: the next oligopoly

With the media frenzy that surrounded generative AI in summer 2023, pressure quickly mounted for governments to step up and take some action to protect users from existential threats (covered in more detail in the next chapter). The EU went legislative: doubling down on their efforts to negotiate an AI Act that was agreeable to all 27 member states, finally managing to get a draft agreement over the line in December of that year and approving the draft text a couple of months later. The UK – keen to portray itself as an intellectual global convener of technology innovation – set about bringing 28 nations together to discuss the future of AI safety and foundation models and pledged funding to start designing an environment where (largely academic) innovation might fuel growth. The United States took a federated, free market approach, encouraging sectoral regulators to police their own AI use-cases, while offering key commercial players the opportunity to step up and lead the way on AI safety, security and trust.

So it is no coincidence that when seven of the leading lights in artificial intelligence – including Google, Microsoft, Meta, Amazon and OpenAI – announced at the White House in July 2023 that they would implement voluntary guardrails for their future AI products, Microsoft's president Brad Smith summed up the agreement in three words: 'safe, secure, trustworthy'.[1]

Such a show of public-spirited solidarity from Google, Microsoft, Meta and Amazon caught many by surprise. Campaigners have pointed out that the tech industry has a history of failing to adhere to pledges on self-regulation and *The New Yorker* wrote: 'There are three ways to greet the announcement: with hope that it could protect people from the most dangerous aspects of AI, with scepticism that it will, or with cynicism that it is a ploy by Big Tech to avoid governmental regulation of real consequence.'

Then came the announcement from four of the same players – Google, Microsoft, OpenAI and Anthropic – of the creation of the Frontier Model Forum,[2] which would 'bring the tech sector together in advancing AI responsibly and tackling the challenges so that it benefits all of humanity'. The main objectives of the forum were stated as:

1. Advancing AI safety research to promote responsible development of frontier models, minimise risks, and enable independent, standardised evaluations of capabilities and safety.
2. Identifying best practices for the responsible development and deployment of frontier models, helping the public understand the nature, capabilities, limitations and impact of the technology.
3. Collaborating with policymakers, academics, civil society and companies to share knowledge about trust and safety risks.
4. Supporting efforts to develop applications that can help meet society's greatest challenges, such as climate change mitigation and adaptation, early cancer detection and prevention, and combatting cyber threats.

The creation of the Forum provoked instant media criticism, notably from the *Financial Times* and *Washington Post*, which wrote: 'For years policymakers have said that Silicon Valley can't be trusted to craft its own guardrails, following more than a decade of privacy lapses, threats to democracies around the world and incidents that endangered children online.'

Who are the most powerful AI players?

The ten most influential companies in AI have earned their places by publicly driving forward technological development in artificial intelligence and machine learning, principally because – for nine of them anyway – technology is their core business activity.

Alphabet (Google), **Meta** (Facebook), **X** (Twitter) and **Amazon** are all digital native companies, bred from and for the internet age. They survive and thrive because of the ways they have developed of interpolating and manipulating vast quantities of data. Each of them enjoys a near monopolistic market position, with hundreds of millions of global users, and each devotes a great deal of activity to learning exactly what each person wants, so their platforms can keep learning and delivering as required.

Although launched in 2015, **OpenAI** appeared in the public consciousness almost overnight in November 2022 with the launch of Chat GPT, only to grow and progress with alarming efficiency, all but abandoning its non-profit status and reaching a $157bn valuation within two years. Its place in the top ten is earned by its creation of platforms which have captured imaginations and demonstrated a giant technological leap. The other reason for its influence is its wunderkind CEO, Sam Altman, who makes headlines almost as frequently as his company does (he was removed from his post and reinstated by the board in under a week, he has both asked for faster regulation of AI and warned that OpenAI may cease trading in the EU if its legislation proves too prescriptive). In 2023, he launched World Coin, a blockchain-based crypto token side-hustle, which offers humans a digital identity, but can only be verified by allowing

OpenAI to perform a retinal scan. Millions of users signed up, despite World Coin's privacy policy giving no assurances about not sharing retinal scan data with governments or commercial entities.

Microsoft, IBM and **Apple,** while not digital natives, are the most successful and resilient of the previous generation of Big Tech corporations and have maintained (or enhanced) their market positions through constant innovation, creating not just the hardware needed to access the internet, but also the software and slick interfaces that keep improving the seamlessness of customers' experiences, largely through AI acquisitions and in-house product development. **Nvidia,** established in 1993, is slightly younger than the others, but gained its place at the top table because of its importance in the semiconductor and supercomputing arms race. Indeed, Nvidia spent much of 2024 vying for 'most valuable company' since it joined the $3tn market cap club with Apple and Microsoft, with the three firms regularly unseating each other at the top of the stock market.

Accenture may not be considered 'Big Tech' in the traditional sense, but the Irish-American business consulting firm is working to position itself as the 'go-to' partner for businesses with complex digital transformation challenges, becoming the largest acquirer of AI startups outside of the United States. Accenture is a determined player – and policy influencer – in the artificial intelligence landscape, and made headlines in 2023 by pledging to invest a further $3bn in the technology, saying it would double the global headcount of its AI practice from 40,000 to 80,000 staff.

In *The Logic of Strategic Assets: From Oil to AI,*[3] researchers Jeffrey Ding and Allan Dafoe examined the similarities between AI and some of history's earlier general purpose technologies, by applying cumulative-strategic, infrastructure-strategic or dependency-strategic logics. In each of these cases, first-mover advantage for the 'early principals' translated into decades-long oligopolistic scenarios. To expand on the work by Ding and

Dafoe, it could be argued that Big Tech is currently deploying the same playbook:

Logic	Description	Examples	Years	Early Principals	Current dominants
Cumulative – strategic	Have high barriers to entry due to first-mover dynamics, incumbency advantages, economies of scale, or other cumulative dynamics.	Digital Social Networks	2006–present	Twitter (X), Meta, LinkedIn, MySpace	Twitter (X), Meta, LinkedIn
Infrastructure – strategic	Generates (diffuse) positive spillovers across the national economy or military system. These are often fundamental technologies that upgrade the national technological system.	Electricity	1880–1925	Edison (now GE), London Electric Supply Corporation (subsequently merged, nationalised, then privatised. Now E.On)	All global conglomerates whose roots can be traced to the electrification boom
Dependency – strategic	Supply characterised by extramarket dynamics and few substitutes.	Integrated circuits	1980–present	Texas Instruments, IBM, Intel, AMD, Siemens, SGS-Thompson (now ST)	Texas Instruments, IBM, Intel, AMD, Siemens, ST, Nvidia

Over the last couple of years, these Big Tech firms have invested billions of dollars on in-house generative AI projects, or in fast moving startups like OpenAI (Microsoft and Nvidia); Anthropic (Amazon and Google) and Inflection AI (Nvidia and Microsoft). Regulators in the USA, UK and Europe soon opened competition investigations into the companies concerned.

It is also worth bearing in mind that Google, Microsoft and Amazon collectively hold a 65% market share in cloud computing (with hosting often a key component of the value of their investments in AI startups), as significant processing and storage capabilities are needed to power a lot of artificial intelligence, particularly large language models).

The AI Index report from Stanford University found that Google and OpenAI's LLMs are particularly thirsty when it comes to computing power: OpenAI's GPT-4 used an estimated $78m worth of compute to train, while Google's Gemini Ultra cost $191m for compute.[4] As the models become increasingly complex, cloud computing is seen as the key enabler of development in this space. The other key market players are Oracle and IBM in the west and Alibaba in China.

Add to this the impact of the US–China semiconductor trade war, which helped Nvidia seize somewhere between 80–90% of the global market share in AI processing chips. Campaigners hope regulators will keep an eye on this dominance: Nvidia's proposed takeover of UK-based chip-maker Arm was blocked by America's Federal Trade Commission. The conglomerate isn't short of competitors: other key players, including Intel, are still investing billions into specific chip development for artificial intelligence. In such a fast-growing market and with government subsidies to play for in many countries, that market dominance could change in relatively short order.

Big Tech's shopping spree

While regulators are likely to keep one eye on Big Tech's hunger for ownership of the most high-profile AI startups, various investment rounds have already diluted their ownership – in many cases, between multiple Big Tech players – which should keep competition watchdogs at bay for now. What may be of more interest to regulators would be whether Big Tech's notoriously anticompetitive behaviours (like platforms and browsers giving far more preference to one model over another) filter through to the startups they are so heavily invested in, as new marketplaces and areas for business opportunity evolve.

None of these 'influencers' are new to the artificial intelligence space. The illustration below shows the acquisition spree that Apple, Accenture, Alphabet, Microsoft and Meta went on between 2016 and 2020.

It is worth noting that the most significant purchase from a UK perspective was Google's acquisition of advanced data analytics research firm DeepMind in 2014, the company most often cited as the main reason the UK deserves a place in the AI debate. However, as commentator James Phillips notes, 'Without DeepMind the UK's share of the citations amongst the top 100 recent AI papers drops from 7.84% to just 1.86%.'[5] To clarify, the grid below only shows outright acquisitions, not significant investments, such as Microsoft's $13bn multi-year investment in OpenAI.

Acquirer	2016	2017	2018	2019	2020
Apple	Emotient; Tuplejump Software; Turi; Flyby Media; Glimpse	Lattice Data; Pop Up Archive; RealFace; Shazam Entertainment; DeskConnect; SensoMotoric; Regaind	Asaii; Silk Labs; Spektral Aps	Drive.ai; Laserlike; PullString; Spectral Edge; Lighthouse AI	Inductiv; Subverse; Voysis; XNOR.AI; Vilynx
Accenture	Ops Rules Partners; Tecnilogica	Clear head; Genfour; Media Hive; Search Tech; LabAnswer Govt.; Endgame	kogentix; Real Time Analytics	BRIDGE Energy Group; Pragsis Technologies; Sutter Mills	Clarity Solution Group; ESR Labs; N3; Salt Solutions

Acquirer	2016	2017	2018	2019	2020
Google (Alphabet)	Eyefluence; Moodstocks; Speaktoit; Anvato; Apigee	Halli Labs Private; Kaggie; AI Matter	Terraform Labs; Xively; Socratic.org	Superpod	Looker Data Science; SolveBot
Microsoft	Genee; TouchType	Maluuba; Hexadite	Bonsai AI; Lobe AI; Semantic Machines; XOXCO	PromoteIQ; jClarity	CyberX; Orions Systems
Facebook (Meta)	FacioMetrics	Ozio; fayteq	Bloomsbury AI; Confirm.io	CTRL-Labs; GrokStyle; Servicefriend	Scape Technology

Data from CBInsights shows that over 1,000 AI businesses were bought by more than 800 acquirers between 2010 and 2021.[6] Over 90% made just one acquisition. During that period, Apple, Accenture, Alphabet, Microsoft and Meta collectively bought 80 firms.

Not quite in the top ten, but still of note, there are a few companies in this space who keep a slightly lower profile, but are increasingly influential. Chief among these is **Palantir**, which specialises in public sector AI projects for various government departments including the MoD, NHS and Cabinet Office in the UK and the United States Department of Defense. According to GlobalData,[7] as of December 2022, Palantir had taken on £98.34m worth of UK government contracts since 2015 and its influence as a sectoral expert should not be overlooked.

Also worth mentioning are enterprise cloud players **Salesforce** (which partners strategically with innovative startups, high-potential scale-ups and massive enterprise firms, including America's largest employer, Walmart), **Cisco**, **Servicenow** and **Intel**, who have acquired more than 30 AI startups between them since 2010.

It is no coincidence that six of the most influential AI players – Alphabet, Amazon, Apple, Meta, Microsoft and Nvidia – also rank in the world's top ten global tech companies by revenue. The *Wall Street Journal* described Microsoft as 'the world's most aggressive amasser of AI talent, tools and technology'.

Given their level of investment over the last decade and their undoubted technical expertise, it is no surprise that these companies are invited to contribute so frequently to the development of public policy. Google, for example, has done well to establish itself as a participant in both the UK government's Digital Skills Council and AI Council, as well as similar high level steering groups in other countries.

Complementors, not competitors

'Competition should not be for a share of the market, but to expand the market,' said statistician and management consultant W. Edwards Deming. Which seems a reasonable guiding philosophy for Big Tech players right now.

In its market analysis, Fortune Business Insights wrote: 'Key players in the global market are enriching their partner ecosystem to gain a competitive advantage... to develop new opportunities by building new solutions together; generate revenue by selling together; expand their presence and share marketing strategies.'

As an example, platform provider Servicenow announced in 2023 it had launched an 'AI Lighthouse' collaboration for enterprise customers, with Accenture bringing the consulting expertise and Nvidia providing the supercomputing capability.

As companies in this space build reputations for niche capabilities, we will undoubtedly see far more collaborations between enterprise firms with different specialisms and customer reach. The biggest obstacle for them will be data residency – working out who holds the data, in which jurisdiction and for what purposes – as data crossing borders is a constant compliance headache for most major enterprise corporations. Of course, a great way to ease concerns would be if those same providers were part of a coalition where all AI development was responsible, reliable and standardised...

Big Tech as gatekeepers

There is growing consternation in political circles over these collaborations and how effective they actually are. *Politico* compared recent moves to self-regulate to those announced by social media companies (including Facebook and Twitter) in the wake of voter manipulation accusations in the 2016 election cycles: 'Suddenly, tech companies were eager to build out their own trust and safety teams to mitigate potential harm. They also warned policymakers that because this stuff was really complicated (it wasn't), it was best to leave it to internal experts who knew exactly what they were doing. Cue six-plus years of social media chaos; rival corporate transparency projects that are still not comparable; and a current winding down of these in-house teams in the wake of social media's financial difficulties.'

But just as there is a chance that moves to self-regulate will follow the same pattern as before and achieve nothing, there is also a viable risk to other businesses that the members of the Frontier Model Forum will use their positions, power, expertise and influence to lay down benchmarks and guidelines that only the members can successfully meet. They have every business incentive to climb the ladder and pull it up behind them, effectively creating their own 'quality standard' for 'safe, secure, trustworthy' AI, which only they and their paying customers can hope to display.

Bear in mind that just three companies have already shored up an oligopolistic position when it comes to media spend: Amazon, Alphabet and Meta collectively bank more than 50% of total global digital advertising revenue.[8] Given the stranglehold that those companies exert over the internet and media landscapes (and the high barriers to entry they've built to ward off any would-be competitors), their reach is greater than most nation-states, so a subsequent campaign about the dangers of non-compliant AI would be entirely plausible (and who better to decide what 'safe, secure, trustworthy' look like?).

How does this oligopoly impact non-tech firms?

Some of the 400 biggest companies in the UK are already heavily (if quietly) invested in making artificial intelligence and other emerging technologies work for them, at their pace, meeting their problems, improving their businesses, in their way. Many, many more are at much earlier stages on their data transformation journeys, but they will need the technologies – and the regulatory environments they operate in – to be fit for purpose, so they can protect their productivity, their people and their profits, for the next hundred years.

Because of the global nature of their businesses, they own the world's largest and most complicated data sets and are likely to be the most impacted by regulatory change in multiple jurisdictions, yet they are rarely consulted by policymakers on the future of data-driven technologies like artificial intelligence. An educated guess would be that as much as 75% of the world's data is held in proprietary silos by enterprise-scale organisations. While it is impossible to find an absolute number, several sources in both government and industry agreed that this was not an unreasonable estimate.

Paradoxically, they also suffer from a lack of access to their data and the ability to unlock value from it. The first problem for most of these firms is data: they don't have enough control over it. The data they do control is not of the right quality, they suffer from significant issues of data scarcity and data bias, they don't have access to enough of the right resources and even if they do, they aren't able to define a systemic problem clearly enough to be able to generate an effective answer, unless they collaborate with the rest of the integrated system facing into that problem.

The second challenge isn't to do with technology at all. It's cultural. It's about how organisations get themselves into a position, culturally and operationally, where they're able to realise value from applying machine learning techniques to industrial problems. Businesses are not going to be able to generate value from the work that they're doing if the cultures in those organisations don't adapt.

In innovation workshops and round tables I've run, large businesses are sometimes referred to as U-Boats, while startups are commonly seen as minnows. This popular characterisation of them being 'slow to move' obscures a truth that many of them are spending tens or hundreds of millions of pounds on developing cutting-edge technologies to ensure a competitive advantage in fast-moving industries.

The Big Tech companies currently advising governments and policymakers, through strategic advisory firms and lobbying organisations as well as positions on committees, are enterprise technology builders who want to sell product. They are all relatively young companies with a limited appreciation of the complexities of being a multi-generational incumbent with legacy data. And their experience is very firmly rooted in tertiary, or service industries.

When you look at the most influential of these, each was established in the business-to-business (B2B) or business-to-consumer (B2C) service sectors. Accenture is a professional services firm, Microsoft, IBM, Nvidia and Apple all started (and are still actively involved) in the consumer electronics space. The others, like Google and Meta, are consumer software providers by background.

A common misconception is that UK businesses don't make anything anymore. The country's manufacturing heyday of the 19th century Industrial Revolution may be far behind us, but half of the biggest firms are still operating very successfully in primary or secondary industries, including:

- Engineering
- Mining
- Oil
- Manufacturing
- Minerals
- Chemicals
- Aerospace
- Electrical
- Defence
- Pharmaceutical
- Energy
- Automotive
- Utilities
- Life Sciences
- Steel

Overview of the UK's 400 largest companies, divided by market segment

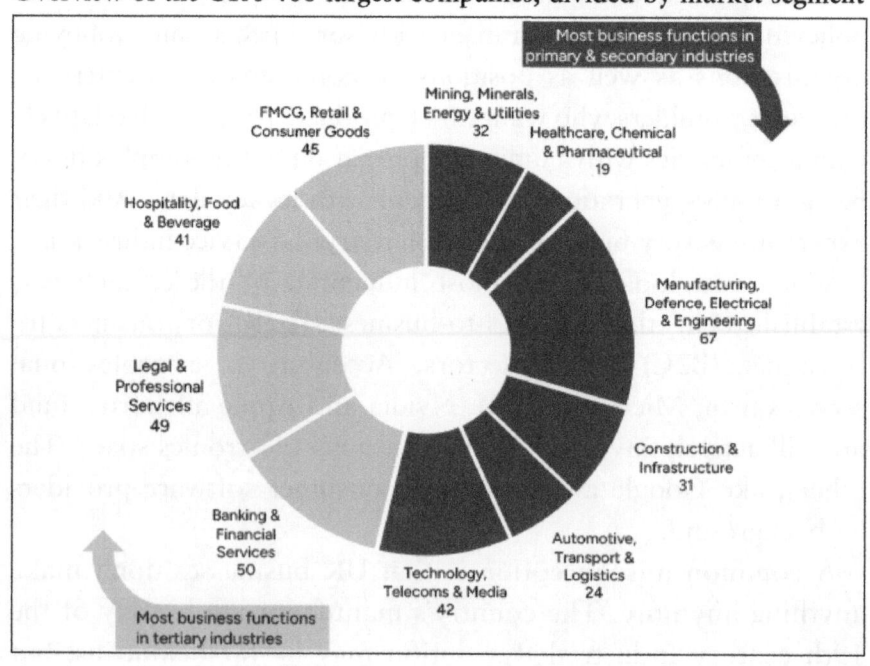

One Chief Technology Officer I interviewed estimated her business has spent over £100m in the last few years on AI development. But she told us that advanced data analytics processes were now so well embedded across every aspect of 'business as usual' – manufacture, customer service and procurement – that much of the true AI and ML cost didn't come from her balance sheet any longer, so it had become impossible – and unnecessary – to track the spend effectively, beyond novel projects and deployments.

But for every enterprise-scale business in the UK that has already invested £100m or more on deploying artificial intelligence and machine learning, there are another ten who are still £100m away from being able to harness the power of this game-changing technology. And they will be faced with the choice of building it in-house, or outsourcing it.

In some of these larger businesses, there are – right now in the 21st century – entire treasure troves of data, held in technical specifications, hand-drawn on well-thumbed paper that cannot be analysed or understood by any off-the-shelf computer vision programme which has been trained on generic, available data.

For the most part, these companies cannot unlock the value of ML or advanced data analytics by buying a 'white box' AI product from an enterprise software provider, because their needs are niche and difficult to understand. They cannot be catered for by a startup with five years' experience building apps in Cupertino, California.

Where will economic growth show up?

According to Fortune Business Insights analysis, the global AI market is due to more than quadruple in size by 2030, to a value of over $2tn.[9] Current estimates are that the top 30 technology businesses operating in this space have a combined 35% ($150bn) market share, the majority of which (about $107bn-worth) is shared by the top twelve (the top ten 'influencers', plus Salesforce and Anthropic).

In June 2024, Apple finally unveiled its long-awaited AI offering in partnership with, of course, OpenAI. Apple Intelligence's unique selling point was that it would deliver personalised AI services while honouring the iPhone maker's mission to keep customers' sensitive data secure. To do so without sacrificing privacy, the company said it had built a new way to handle sensitive data in the cloud.

The announcement boosted its stock market valuation by over $300bn. But, more interestingly, it was an early sign that generative AI was ready to accelerate through the AI 'hype cycle', from the experimentation phase to the mass adoption phase. While Microsoft took the leap and was prepared to make a few snafus in being the first to market as the earliest corporate adopter of OpenAI's technology, this move by Apple showed not just deployment, but a considered holistic integration of the tech into already desirable new products, firmly with a view on how to improve the customer experience.

As Axios reported at the time, 'Apple isn't a "picks and shovels" company like Nvidia, the stock market darling of the first phase of the AI hype cycle. It isn't selling AI chips or AI consultants or Large Language Models or even AI training data. It's selling phones, which will be better thanks to AI.' Consumer confidence in Apple as a designer and manufacturer of silky-smooth hardware and software will go a long way to embedding AI into people's daily lives.

Brynjolfsson *et al* predicted in their 2018 paper *The Productivity J Curve*: 'If the trajectory of previous general purpose technologies holds, the effective diffusion of AI will take decades and many complementary innovations.'[10] Developments like Apple's suggest that this type of technology is on an accelerated trajectory, which is likely to continue as generative AI becomes more seamlessly integrated into the things people do. As tech commentator Melissa Heikkilä put it: 'The AI revolution hasn't felt like one. Instead, it's been a slow slide toward marginal efficiency gains. I see more autocomplete functions in my email and word processing applications, and Google Docs now offers more ready-made templates. They are not groundbreaking features, but they are also reassuringly inoffensive.'

The wider economic impact arguments are harder to predict and quantify, but as long as a handful of technology companies are gobbling up talent and acquiring bleeding edge technologies, they are actively offshoring intellectual property and increasing their market share. While it is a reassuring capitalist wisdom that 'companies grow, therefore the economy grows', technology usage is entirely borderless and it is hard to see how the AI market growing to $2tn benefits all geographies equally, when most of the algorithms and training models driving this growth are domiciled in California, with its innovation-friendly tax regime.

Analysts at Deutsche Bank reported the combined market cap of the so-called 'magnificent seven' stocks (Alphabet, Amazon, Apple, Meta, Microsoft, Nvidia and Tesla) outstrip those of all listed companies in almost every G20 country, making them equivalent to being the second-largest country stock exchange in the world.[11] Nvidia stock, often seen as a proxy for AI demand, added more than $1.2tn to its market cap in under a year, with Goldman Sachs analysts calling it 'the most important stock on planet earth' in 2024. While this looks like a good news story for the United States, there are concerns the country may be becoming overly dependent on its highly acquisitive technology sector: Morgan Stanley's Counterpoint Global pointed out a concentration risk in the rapidly rising US market valuations, which 'were responsible for more than one-half of the S&P 500's gain of 26.3 percent in 2023'.[12]

The truth about market dominance

If current estimates are correct, the top ten hold about 25% of the AI market share, while over 55% is held by many thousands of smaller businesses and an unknowable number of large corporates for whom data is not a core activity. Big Tech players have incredible reach and their products and services are used by billions of people every day, which gives them considerable brand equity, but despite hype and perceptions, they are not yet dominant.

While generative AI receives the most media attention, in academic circles, industrial AI sits firmly within a space called Deep Technology (DeepTech): the development of intellectual property and technology solutions based on substantial scientific or engineering challenges. Because of the age and industrial heritage of so many UK corporates, IP intensive industries account for £300bn per year, according to the Intellectual Property Office (IPO), over a quarter of the country's domestic output.

Because of its complexity, there a lack of understanding – among investors, the public and most business executives – about where the opportunities lie to unlock value and economic growth. As the IPO put it in its report, *Intellectual property and investment in Artificial Intelligence*:[13] 'The UK is seen as too small a market to scale-up and too hard to get the larger rounds of investment needed for major long-term growth. Many young companies choose early exit or moving to the USA.'

With around three quarters of corporate data sets held in-house by the largest businesses, it is not possible to design solutions to problems without access to enterprise data. The level of in-house tech development and deployment is difficult to discover and challenging to measure in a universal way. However, having conducted the first major research project to try and establish a baseline in the UK, it has been possible to see that – across all market segments – significant investment is underway and delivering enormous value to the companies using it well.

As noted in research from the International Data Corporation (IDC),[14] the potential for growth in enterprise-focused data innovations is twice the scale of that in the consumer data space.

It is in large corporates, with their vast data repositories, where the greatest value is waiting to be unlocked.

The future of emerging technology – the products available, the range of problems they solve, the way they are regulated, the ethics of their deployment – are being largely influenced by the ten or so companies that have spent the most money in the last decade buying exciting startups with algorithms that can be easily applied to the most generic 80% of data problems in the business world.

The experts I have spoken to are convinced that the greatest potential economic value lies in the much harder-to-reach 20%.

5

Capitalism vs. AI policymakers

While technology advancements have been a consistent force in the workplace for the last 150 years, upending and reimagining the way people do their jobs and shaping the skills needed to succeed in competitive environments, they have never moved at such an incredible pace.

Although the rise of the personal computer began to grab hold of the public imagination with the rapid development of information technology in the 1980s, it wasn't until the late 1990s that the subsequent IT productivity boom arrived, even though it was based on technologies developed a decade earlier. 'You can see the computer age everywhere but in the productivity statistics,' economist Robert Solow observed in 1987.

This was in large part because for companies, competition in the early computer age required massive capital investment in hardware and infrastructure. This did mean that widespread adoption of the 'world-wide web' a few years later was able to move exponentially faster (even if dial-up internet speeds were not), because it integrated information through the browsers already on most knowledge workers' desktops.

It is easy to take the pace of change for granted as nearly half of people in the workforce today are under 40.[1] But the majority of people who run these organisations are in their 40s, 50s or 60s. I'm 45 years old and I am just about old enough to have lived through this transition of ready internet availability: in my first office job, I remember it was my turn to 'check the email' on Fridays; we only had one computer with an email account and we would take turns to check it once a day. It really wasn't that long ago that you couldn't run a business without a fax machine: the second company I worked for had no external internet, but did run an integrated stock system, which communicated over telephone lines. However, a huge amount of our work was still paper-based and depended on the regular sending and receiving of faxes.

During this time, I launched my first business, which was an online directory of art galleries across the UK. This was before the advent of Google or the term 'search engine' and managing the directory was an intensely manual process. By the time I joined the third company I worked for, the office game had changed completely, with connected personal computers on every desk, each wired up to the internet. Email had – almost overnight – become the principal means of communicating with customers. This process took just four years.

The reason the world seems to be moving much faster now is that most computational processes can be automatically accessed through a browser on any number of personal devices: laptops, tablets and phones all give the user instant access to a world of information (and disinformation for that matter). Implementing AI-driven work processes no longer requires the same level of upfront investment in equipment that earlier waves of technology needed. Much as with 'electronic mail', most knowledge workers already sit at computers all day, so access is both seamless and necessary in order to compete.

There are many other types of industrial technology we could consider here – Internet of Things, Virtual Reality, Cloud, Blockchain – but I will focus on AI because (a) that's the research I've been doing, and (b) artificial intelligence in its broadest sense intersects all of the others. It is technology which underpins a way of working rather than a system, platform or interface. It is the new set of rules we must all learn, much as we once had to learn to send a message by issuing a send instruction to firstname.lastname@company.com instead of putting a stamp on an envelope.

As analysts at McKinsey put it: 'AI is the new steam. Hear us out: steam power, mechanised engines, and coal supply chains powered the First Industrial Revolution. The Fourth Industrial Revolution is already under way, but the efflorescence of AI has bent the S-curve for advanced manufacturing such that leaders are achieving truly transformative growth.' [2]

18 months in the Artificial Intelligence arms race

Spurred on by a sudden exponential leap in technological capability (and the headlines it generated), western policymakers have tried to work at a considerable pace to implement guardrails to protect their citizens from perceived threats posed by artificial intelligence. This flurry of activity over a remarkably short time (18 months between November 2022 and April 2024) provides a fascinating snapshot into the varying approaches of western governments, regulators and policymakers...

The UK government consulted on, and published, its *AI Regulation: a pro-innovation approach*[3] white paper, disbanded its AI Council and began forming first a Foundation Model Taskforce, then an AI Safety Institute; pledged £1.5bn to build the next generation of supercomputers and tens of millions of pounds in funding to support sectoral regulators and new regional AI research hubs; and hosted the first global AI Safety Summit in November 2023, bringing together leading AI nations, technology companies, researchers and civil society groups to drive action on the safe and responsible development of frontier AI around the world. The impression coming out of the UK was that from a policy perspective, it wanted to nurture opportunity, research and startups, hoping to replicate its success with fintechs a decade earlier. It clearly hoped to punch above its intellectual weight as a global hub of innovation and academic advancement in AI. To an extent, this worked, as public recognition followed. Within a year, publications like Air Street Capital's annual State of AI Report added a 'safety' metric, saying 'governments around the world emulate the UK in building up state capacity around AI safety, launching institutes and studying critical national infrastructure for potential vulnerabilities'.[4]

The EU legislature, after two and a half years of negotiation, agreed to introduce a sweeping new AI Act,[5] with binding rules on transparency and ethics, intended to force technology firms to be a lot more transparent about what data they use to train their models, with punitive fines for non-compliance, between 1.5% and 7% of a firm's global turnover; the European Commission brought into law a new Digital Markets Act to encourage a level playing field for European companies to compete in tech innovation; and the EU began setting up a new European AI Office, to coordinate compliance, implementation and enforcement of the new legislation. Meanwhile, Europe also issued Meta with the largest ever GDPR fine – €1.2bn – for data residency breaches. The overall vibe from Brussels was a sense of urgent, structured, regulated approach, concerned with misuse of power and technology – particularly facial recognition – and a protection of citizen freedoms.

The Unites States administration created a blueprint for its AI Bill of Rights;[6] published a National AI Research and Development Strategic Plan;[7] set up a National AI Advisory Committee (NAIAC); and then President Biden issued an Executive Order to minimise technology bias, which outlined a distributed approach to AI policy, encouraging different government agencies to craft their own rules. The flavour of domestic AI policy emerging from Washington was one which was decentralised and broadly friendly to the technology industry, with an emphasis on best practice and an approach which regulated each sector on a case-by-case basis. On the international stage, as well as participating in the AI Safety Summit, it signed a joint AI safety risk partnership with the UK, outlining how to share technical expertise, talent and knowledge.

Meanwhile, over the course of the same 18 months...

OpenAI released ChatGPT-3 then GPT-4 for text, as well as DALL-E for image generation (and filed a patent application for GPT-5 to include voice recognition); launched a GPT app marketplace and an early text-to-video programme called Sora, which turned short prompts into detailed, high-definition movie clips; CEO Sam Altman was briefly ousted, with rumours rapidly spreading that OpenAI had managed to create an AI system that could solve complex mathematical problems, which would be a giant leap towards the development of artificial general intelligence (AGI), capable of advanced reasoning.

Google rushed the release of its problematic chatbot Bard before taking time to launch an AI writing assistant, Gemini, to be rolled out across the entire Google estate (including Chrome). It also launched both PaLM2, a large language model with 'advanced reasoning capabilities', and RT-2, the first robot to learn and 'think by itself'. Its London-based development lab, DeepMind, then launched a similar vision language model called AutoRT, and announced its team had developed an AI capable of solving sophisticated geometry problems. DeepMind founder Demis Hassabis's drug discovery spinoff, Isomorphic Labs, also announced two new strategic collaborations with major pharmaceutical companies Eli Lilly and Novartis, worth nearly $3bn, to discover potential new treatments using AI.

Microsoft's significant partnership with, and investment in, OpenAI raised its market valuation so steeply that it spent many months vying with Apple (and then Nvidia) to be the world's most valuable company. It added ChatGPT to its search engine Bing and launched 365 Copilot, its AI agent capable of learning from corporations' internal data, which opened up access to OpenAI's generative AI technology within existing software programmes, while also offering more seamless ways for non-coders to develop software.

Meta launched new social platform Threads with plans to use 30 chatbot personae to drive engagement as well as releasing three versions of its own open-source LLM (LLaMa) in quick succession. In January 2024, twenty years after Facebook pioneered the new social media landscape, CEO Mark Zuckerberg jumped on the Artificial General Intelligence (AGI) bandwagon, announcing a new goal to build open-source 'full general intelligence', by blending its AI research teams, strengthening its computing infrastructure and building out the next version of its LLaMa model.

More than 180 AI startups were acquired by major corporates, mostly US enterprise technology firms, some of whom, with the apparent backing of the White House, announced a pathway to self-regulation.

Elon Musk completed his $44bn purchase of one of the world's biggest social media platforms, rebranded it as X, launched a new company, X.ai, to be built on data from Twitter and his other businesses (including Neuralink, which successfully implanted the first brain chips in test patients, SpaceX, whose subsidiary Starlink became the largest commercial satellite operator in space, and Tesla, which built its own supercomputer, called Dojo). Musk announced an intention to develop an 'everything app' to rival China's Tencent, but with far greater AI capability.

Policy in this space moved much faster than usual, but Big Tech continued to move at lightning speed during the same period. 'AI is one of the most important things humanity is working on. It is more profound than electricity or fire,' said Sundar Pichai, CEO at Alphabet, Google's parent company.

Incidentally, it was only after this 18-month period of technological advancement and legislative positioning that a period of reckoning for Big Tech players began, as regulators started to flex their new muscles. In a single month (June 2024):

- The EU announced it would take action against Apple, linked to the company's compliance with the Digital Markets Act. Danish politician Margrethe Vestager declared the technology giant was the first Big Tech firm to have been found to breach the bloc's new competition rules, by failing to allow smaller rival companies in the App Store to compete effectively; a separate (but connected) investigation was also launched into the App Store's terms and conditions; the Commission then went after Microsoft, saying it had likely broken antitrust rules by linking Teams to its wider portfolio software products;
- In the US, just as it announced it had started building an in-house competitor to OpenAI, Microsoft came under scrutiny from the Federal Trade Commission, which launched an investigation into its relationship with OpenAI, as well as looking into whether it structured its investment in Inflection AI in such a way as to avoid a government antitrust review of the deal;
- Vestager then said the Commission would begin to 'take third party views' on the partnership between Microsoft and OpenAI, as well as one announced between Google and Samsung.

This also began a period of reckoning about the quality of data polluting the web and, for many, 2024 became the year that artificial intelligence ate its own tail. Researchers at Amazon Web Services found that over half the sentences on the global internet had already been machine-translated into other languages, warning this could have severe consequences for the quality of data used to train future AI models.[8]

With many of today's largest AI models actively scraping the internet as their database – and publishing the outputs back onto the internet – a research paper published in *Nature* found that within just nine iterations, the outputs had degraded to the point of total collapse, according to co-author Zakhar Shumaylov, a University of Cambridge AI researcher.[9] Without being careful about data inputs, he said, 'things will always, provably, go wrong'.

Demonstrating model collapse in the research, the team took a pre-trained LLM and fine-tuned it by using Wikipedia entries, before instructing the resulting model to generate similar Wikipedia-style articles. The next generation of the model started with the same pre-trained LLM, was fine-tuned on the articles created by its predecessor. They compared the outputs of each generation against the original and saw total degradation to 'gibberish' within just a few iterations.

The study also found that subsequent generations of the model 'forgot' the information mentioned least frequently, so that results became more homogenous. Co-author Ilia Shumailov, from the University of Oxford, pointed out that this is a bad omen for marginalised groups or anomalous events, making it difficult for LLM-generated text to represent all groups (and opinions) fairly.

Following this, in September 2024, Wordfreq, a major Python library which looked up the frequencies of words in many languages, announced it would close down because 'generative AI has polluted the data'. The long running open-source data project scraped the internet to analyse how humans use language, but found that since 2021, there had been too much AI-generated text online to make any reliable analyses.

Trust, Fear and Democracy

In a survey conducted across the USA, UK and Europe in June and July 2023,[10] almost one in four (23%) respondents said they had 'no trust at all' that generative AI tools would respect their data privacy. Data protection watchdogs on both side of the

Atlantic are likely to place considerable scrutiny on how firms like Google, OpenAI and Meta utilise personal data as these platforms develop.

Public perceptions of trust around AI applications are hugely variable, but most voters don't want to have to think about algorithms and data ethics. They simply expect their elected representatives to make sure the apps on their smartphones won't try to kill them in their sleep. It is perhaps easier to work out what voters require by eliminating what they **don't want:**

- For them or their children to be endangered by any technology
- To worry about criminals stealing their identity or personal data
- To feel wary using the devices that make their lives more convenient

All of those are plausible, reasonable and pretty universal for anyone living in a 21st century democracy. When more than two billion people headed to the polls in the largest ever number of general elections taking place – over 50% of the world's democracies – in 2024, politicians across the EU, the UK and the United States were quite understandably keen to prioritise legislative activities which satisfied the needs of their constituents.

The three buzz words every politician needs, in order to sum up what they have done (or will do) when legislating technology, are the same three Microsoft's Brad Smith used: **Safe. Secure. Trustworthy.** Most voters, hearing that technology is more safe, secure and trustworthy, will accept that as reasonable and then focus their thoughts on taxes, crime and energy bills as being higher priority issues.

Insofar that the general public understands – or even considers – artificial intelligence, it is the AI of books and movies: existential threats to humanity, robots stealing their jobs and the pervasive nature of CCTV facial recognition, like in the dystopian *Mission: Impossible* movie franchise, which showed an advanced AI, ominously called The Entity, which had gone rogue in search of global domination.

The fears for public safety have been stoked by AI pioneers, among them the 'godfather of AI', Geoffrey Hinton, author and former Googler Mo Gawdat, leading academic Yoshua Bengio and Anthropic CEO Dario Amodei, who all warned American legislators about the 'catastrophic' potential of AI. 'In particular, I am concerned that AI systems could be misused on a grand scale in the domains of cybersecurity, nuclear technology, chemistry, and especially biology,' said Amodei.

It doesn't help that some of the fastest-moving, most popular generative AI models are shrouded in secrecy about how they function, what data sets they are trained on and how they might develop. Partly in response to public and government concerns, OpenAI set up what it called a 'superalignment team' to research the technology's long-term risks. The group was disbanded a few months later, but not before writing a research paper which was published shortly after OpenAI co-founder and Chief Scientist Ilya Sutskever left the business.[11] Rather than quelling concerns, the paper raised more questions about whether even the experts fully understood the implications of what they were building. 'Unlike with most human creations, we don't really understand the inner workings of neural networks,' admitted the authors in an accompanying blog post.

So it is no surprise that policymakers or politicians struggle to gets to grips with the harms and risks posed by AI, to work out when to intervene, how to reach consensus, or what the unexpected downsides of the wrong kind of intervention might be. A survey of 108 members of parliament conducted by the Appraise Network in May 2023 found that while 44% of UK MPs felt optimistic about AI, barely 23% felt they understood the implications for citizens and society (43% did not; 34% said they didn't know).[12]

That study found that only 6% of MPs believed existing regulators had the skills or expertise to regulate artificial intelligence and that nearly half of them agreed that AI is developing too fast to keep up with. This is a relatively new area in public consciousness and the wrong knee-jerk reactions could be potentially disastrous.

Then UK Prime Minister Rishi Sunak said: 'Harnessing the potential of AI provides enormous opportunities to grow our economy, create better-paid jobs and build a better future.' But it isn't all sunny uplands. As Tony Blair and William Hague wrote in their 2023 report, *A New National Purpose*[13] 'AI's unpredictable development, the rate of change and its ever-increasing power mean its arrival could present the most substantial policy challenge we've ever had.' Below I will explore some of these existential risks:

'Robots are coming for my job'

An Ipsos poll in 2023 found that 64% of UK adults felt 'the government should create new regulations or laws to prevent the potential loss of jobs due to AI'.[14] While workers are concerned about artificial intelligence's effects on the long-term sustainability of their jobs, when a technology is being almost seamlessly embedded into processes and devices we use every day, it is impossible to identify what one political party over another could do about it.

The flipside is this: if the people who still have jobs will be dependent on AI to be able to do them, should regulators or politicians even try to slow down the march of technology? A survey by law firm Clifford Chance found that 31% of tech policy influencers believed new AI regulation was likely to be so prescriptive that it would harm innovation.[15] Besides, after four decades of rampant globalism, voters are already accustomed to the idea of their roles being 'offshored' to countries that will do what we won't, for a lower price. That threat seems just as valid, so the jobs argument becomes paradoxical.

'I'm being watched all the time'

This is a central pillar of the European legislative approach to building AI systems. Predictive policing has been banned, except in situations where 'clear human assessment and objective facts' have been used first. Meanwhile, exploiting human vulnerabilities, manipulating people, using sensitive characteristics to categorise them, social scoring (which has been active in China for some time), developing facial recognition databases using CCTV footage or the internet, and enabling emotion recognition in schools or workplaces are now illegal in Europe.

'My life may be at risk from rogue AI'

With AI being increasingly used over the last decade in healthcare and drug discovery settings, from robotic remote surgery assistants to X-ray image recognition, there is a very real set of risks around misdiagnosis, but these uses are (currently) in tightly regulated and well-supervised environments so the risks are relatively small... as long as you're a cisgender white male. Human rights advocates and AI researchers regularly point out harms already being caused in situations where AI systems often disproportionately misdiagnose health issues in Black and brown patients, and women. Policing is another situation frequently flagged up where non-white people are misidentified, arrested and tried with alarming regularity, based on algorithmic interpretations.

'Rogue AI is taking over the world'

'Most of global GDP is mediated in some way through screen-based interfaces, usable by an AI,' said DeepMind co-founder Mustafa Suleyman. With the exponential rise in AI-enabled assistants or chatbots that can browse the internet, nowhere near enough scrutiny has been given to the security of these systems: a classic example of Silicon Valley not learning the lessons from the IoT craze of the mid-2010s, where consumers found their refrigerators being hacked by pranksters. Successful hackers depend on identifying the most vulnerable points in any chain of data custody, so a lack of focus on cyber security makes it relatively easy for bad actors to manipulate AI systems by poisoning them with malicious data. If – as expected – consumers become increasingly dependent on their generative AI 'assistants', seeking advice and delegating life tasks, no one really knows how badly that could end.

'I don't know who or what to trust any more'

The sharp rise in creation of deepfakes (manipulating images and audio to make it look like famous, powerful or vulnerable people said or did things they never said or did), public awareness of AI-powered election misinformation, disinformation and voter meddling have all contributed to a general erosion of trust in what people believe they can see with their own eyes.

This is symptomatic of a broader malaise in many democracies and was put to the test during the marathon 2024 global election cycle. With so many models with different functions being released in such short order, and potentially millions of users pushing the boundaries in how they can be used, it is impossible to predict the impact that generative AI-powered misinformation will have on those democracies in future.

That said, a threat analysis of that year's UK and European election cycle by the Alan Turing Institute found no evidence that AI enabled misinformation meaningfully impacted election results.[16] Researchers identified just 27 viral cases of AI disinformation or deepfakes across the UK, France and EU general elections combined. While still worthy of note and undoubtedly damaging, the 16 confirmed cases in the UK and 11 in France and across the EU were not of the same widespread scale as many feared.

The spotlight will be on governments to do something about deepfakes, in particular their use in targeting women, children and vulnerable people with non-consensual porn, which can be generated by splicing together pornographic images and videos with the faces and bodies of just about anyone whose image exists online. While there have been some incredibly high-profile victims of these malicious activities (chief among them singer Taylor Swift and actor Henry Cavill), there are many thousands of examples of 'revenge porn' ruining the lives of innocent and powerless people.

And it isn't just election-rigging and porn: The *South China Morning Post* reported that scammers managed to swindle $26m out of a multinational company by fooling employees into transferring company funds to five different Hong Kong bank accounts by creating deepfake phone calls purporting to be from the firm's chief financial officer.

What do these existential threats mean for enterprise AI and machine learning?

Most of these existential voter concerns surround the use (or misuse) of generative AI, because that is the technology that has garnered the most column inches in the last couple of years. Most firms will need to invest time and resources into communicating – both internally and externally – the value of embracing change, while educating and embedding a digital mindset and data innovation behaviours across their workforces, so that novel technologies can be rolled out with a minimum of disruption, to deal with the 'robots are coming for my job' concern.

Large, customer-facing businesses (like banks, insurance companies and retailers) will need to think in very deliberate, strategic ways about how they use chatbots and assistants in ethical ways which add value and minimise risk: there should be concerns about what data the foundation models were trained on, the quality of the outputs and the dangers of machines giving out bad advice.

Because this is an emerging area of technology regulation, the majority of the enterprise-scale companies I've spoken to in researching this book have said that their preference is to work with major Big Tech players, rather than building these models in-house or buying from startups, for a simple reason: when regulation inevitably changes, they expect Big Tech firms to be able to pivot quickly and ensure the products they are selling are legally compliant, minimising risk exposure or the chance they may have to scrap or rebuild an expensive system two years down the line. They recognise in the short term, this may be the most expensive option, but in such a fast-changing environment, they see it as the most certain way to ensure their firms' resilience.

When it comes to huge businesses building specific AI for DeepTech purposes, such as supply chain optimisation mapping, or identifying which manufacturing components can be safely recycled, any new regulations are likely to be sector-specific, and focused on preventing harm to employees, passengers or patients. The big risks for these organisations – safety, security, reputational damage, shareholder value – are expected to remain the same as they have always been.

Data analytics and ESG

Understanding the environmental, social and governance impacts of big businesses is a complex space of research. In the first of the cross-industry surveys, I polled board members and senior executives about the challenges they faced interpreting management information, with a specific view on how it related to ESG data within their businesses.

When asked to rate the complexity of their ESG data from one (not at all complex), to five (extremely complex), 83% of the respondents rated the complexity as particularly high:

With 1 being 'not at all complex' and 5 being 'extremely complex', please rate the current complexity of your Sustainability and ESG reporting?

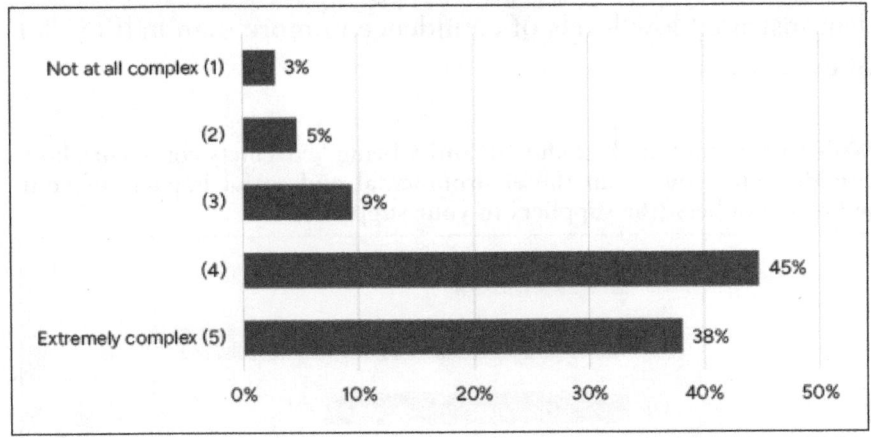

One of the biggest concerns for policymakers – and a lot of enterprise organisations – is understanding the upstream and downstream implications of their sustainability decisions on other participants in their supply chain, as it is relatively easy for large manufacturers, for example, to claim lower carbon emissions, by simply deferring carbon-intensive processes on to their component suppliers. During one interview, an executive from a major high street supermarket told me that they had discovered fruit, picked in Portugal, was being shipped to Argentina to be packaged, before being shipped back to the UK for sale. In a globalised economy, this was marginally cheaper, but I was assured the practice had been stopped when they used data to examine the carbon implications of the decision.

Exploring firms' understanding of their Scope 3 emissions (which relate to the carbon footprint of their supply chain) is an area of interest to policymakers when trying to understand the real impacts of a globalised workforce and supply system. When I surveyed the same group about confidence levels in the environmental and social impacts of their indirect suppliers, again I asked them to rate between one (not at all confident) and five (extremely confident). The results were more ambiguous, with some progress being made in this area, but still demonstrated low levels of confidence in more than half (57%) of executives.

With 1 being 'not at all confident' and 5 being 'extremely confident', how confident are you about the environmental and social impacts of your indirect suppliers (the suppliers to your suppliers)?

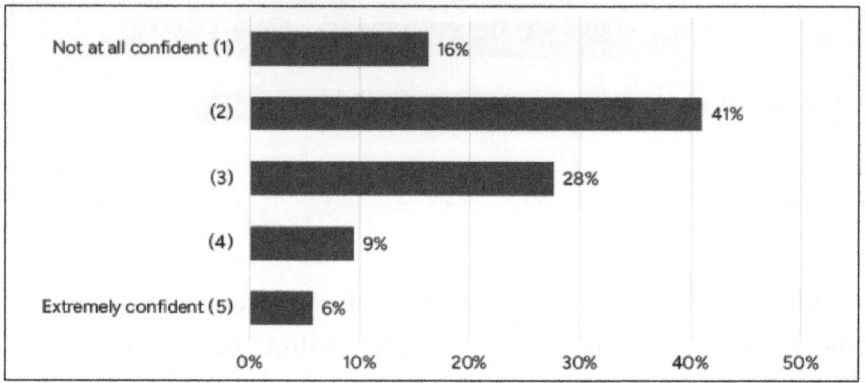

The final question asked concerned the respondents' visibility of their company's Scope 3 carbon emissions. I must put my hands up as a researcher that the question itself was poorly worded and lacked sufficient context.

I think it is important to include this caveat, as the picture it paints is fairly negative... until you consider the variables. For one, while some executives responding to the survey might not personally have any visibility for their Scope 3 emissions, their colleagues may well do. Secondly, Scope 3 emissions are not a regulatory requirement for all firms in all sectors, so for many respondents this question may be irrelevant to meeting their fiduciary requirements. This question-quality failure did not become apparent until I started trying to analyse the data, when far more experienced analysts pointed out my rookie mistake. This was the first survey I conducted for the research project and I promise I got better at it!

However, I include it here for interest:

With 1 being 'no visibility' and 5 being 'total visibility', how much visibility do you currently have of your business's Scope 3 carbon emissions?

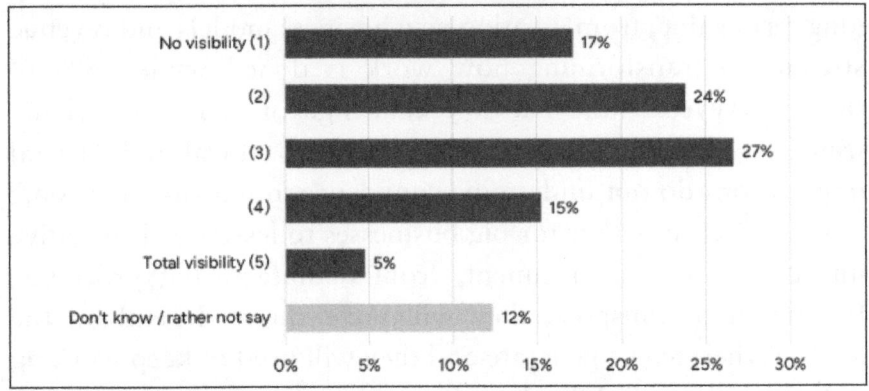

While the findings chime with the charts in the previous chapter around the complexity of management information (taken from the same survey), it is interesting to see how seriously industry leaders are taking their responsibilities to better utilise the data at their disposal to understand the challenges their firms are facing into.

Separately, EY's 2024 report *How can boards convert sustainability from a wish to a winning reality?*[17] focused on the role of governance in sustainable business model innovation. The research (six months after my UK survey) found that NEDs and chairs were not in alignment with executive C-suite leaders when it comes to transformation capability. Non-executives were less confident in the ability of their organisation to drive sustainability transformation, especially with regard to bringing people along on the journey.

- 63% of C-suite executives but only 40% of NEDs and chairs believed they had a highly effective approach when it came to values and culture that reflected sustainability transformation priorities.
- 60% of C-suite executives believed they had a highly effective approach when it came to training (to align the workforce and culture behind sustainability goals), but only 43% of NEDs and chairs agreed.

On the challenges and opportunities for AI, 61% of EY's respondents said, 'AI offers a significant opportunity for driving long-term value, from creating new business models and revenue streams to transforming how work is done,' while 64% of those surveyed said, 'The key challenge of GenAI is driving transformation and growth while ensuring ethical and societal implications do not undermine confidence in our organisation.'

What is clear is that for big businesses to lessen their negative impacts on the environment, from manufacturing processes, logistics and transport, they will increasingly depend on the analysis their teams generate and they will need to keep working to better understand the data they make strategic decisions with.

Getting to grips with generative AI's carbon footprint

Firms focused on climate change and meeting Net Zero commitments may also want to start paying closer attention to the carbon footprint of the models they use.

This is a niche area of study – certainly it doesn't seem to be a major topic for discussion at COP, the planet's go-to forum for climate change – but will be one of increasing importance. Partly, this is because there are no regulatory requirements for technology firms to share information on the carbon footprints generated by training and using their foundation models.

However, in an early piece of research by startup Hugging Face and Carnegie Mellon University,[18] researchers found that generating one image can take as much energy as fully charging a smartphone. Because training the models before products are released is so energy intensive, they reported it took 590 million uses to overtake the energy consumption of training a single multilingual model.

The study also found that using large generative models to create outputs was far more energy intensive than using smaller AI models tailored for specific tasks, and that generating images was significantly more energy intensive than text. The team found that generating 1,000 images with the most powerful AI model used as much CO_2 as driving four miles in a petrol-powered car, while the least carbon-intensive text generation model in the study was responsible for as much carbon dioxide as driving 0.0006 miles.

Further research from Hugging Face and Graphcore demonstrated that training a LLM similar to ChatGPT-3 uses nearly 1,300 megawatt hours of electricity, roughly equal to the annual power consumption of 130 US homes, or streaming over 1,600,000 hours of television on Netflix.[19]

With some of the most popular tools – like ChatGPT – already being used tens of millions of times per day the message from the researchers wasn't to avoid generative AI at all costs, but to start a conversation about 'horses for courses' – that using niche AI, trained on niche data sets, for niche tasks has a far lower carbon footprint than using complex and sophisticated models for relatively simple tasks. However, with Big Tech firms embedding massive language models into everyday applications like Google Docs or Excel, the number of daily uses is expected to rise into the billions and it may already be too late for that conversation.

Goldman Sachs analysts have estimated that carbon emissions from data centres are likely to more than double in the next few years, as a query through ChatGPT needs nearly ten times the electricity used to process a Google search. Google maintains that it used deep learning technology to reduce electricity by 15% across non-IT tasks in its data centres and Microsoft founder Bill Gates thinks AI will do more good than harm in the long run. 'Let's not go overboard on this,' he told the *Guardian*. 'Data centres are, in the most extreme case, a 6% addition [in energy demand] but probably only 2% to 2.5%. The question is, will AI accelerate a more than 6% reduction? And the answer is: certainly.'

In Google's 2024 environmental report,[20] it proudly stated that 'To help minimise our environmental footprint, we've built world-leading efficient infrastructure for the AI era', but went on to admit that 'In 2023, our GHG [greenhouse gas] emissions increased 13% year-on-year, primarily driven by increased data centre energy consumption and supply chain emissions'. Hidden deeper in the report was the admission that the company's emissions had increased by 48% in the previous five years for the same reasons.

Within months, energy provision for AI data centres became a hot topic: the *Wall Street Journal* revealed that the owners of a third of US nuclear plants were in talks with Big Tech players – chief among them Amazon – to provide alternative electricity for AI data centres.[21] Amazon revealed that it planned to spend over $100bn on data centres over the next decade, spending more on data centre infrastructure than on its retail warehousing.

Bill Gates told a conference that Big Tech was 'seriously willing' to pay extra to use clean electricity sources in order 'to say that they're using green energy', as reported by the *Guardian*.[22] Microsoft president Brad Smith had previously admitted that AI-driven data centre energy usage was endangering its 2030 aspiration to become carbon negative. He said 'the moon has moved' due to the firm's AI strategy. Later in the year, Microsoft announced it had signed a 20-year deal to reopen America's Three Mile Island nuclear energy plant to power its AI-driven energy needs.

What role should policymakers play?

I was born and raised in London, I have spent most of my career working in British companies and almost all of the research participants were based in the UK: in global corporations, the studies focused on UK entities and – with seven exceptions – all 300 survey respondents and interviewees were responsible for (and discussing) UK operations. I am plainly not qualified to offer opinions or recommendations on international trade or technology policy, so in this section I will only discuss AI policy from a UK viewpoint.

In January 2022, the UK government's Office for AI published its report on *AI Activity in UK Businesses*,[23] having commissioned Capital Economics to model and report on the current and future use of artificial intelligence by UK firms. Bearing in mind it pre-dates all of the AI advancements at the top of this chapter, the report's five key findings were:

1. Current usage of AI technologies is limited to a minority of businesses; however, it is more prevalent in certain sectors and larger businesses;
2. Different routes are used by businesses to source AI technologies (in-house development, outsourced development and buying enterprise solutions);
3. The scope for increased adoption is large if conditions are right;
4. Future spending on AI technologies is set to increase; and
5. Spending on labour related to AI will increase to support AI technologies' rising prevalence.

The report recognised the correlation between the scale of a company and the complexity of its AI requirements: 'As businesses grow, they are more likely to adopt AI; 68% of large companies have adopted at least one AI technology; Large companies are more likely to adopt multiple AI technologies, around 480 large firms (20%) are currently using four or five AI technologies to assist in their business activities.'

The proportions are higher in enterprise-scale businesses. Gartner (also in 2022) found that one in three firms were applying multiple AI processes in one or more business units,[24] while EY in the same year found that 53% of senior executives had identified data and analytics as their top investment priority over the next two years. [25]

The corporate AI landscape is much broader and more complex than it first appears. Fortune Business Insights estimated the global AI market size to be $428bn, with around two thirds attributable to software and platforms, the other third being hardware and services. It projected the 2030 market to be worth $2,025bn worldwide. If this analysis is correct, there's a trillion and a half to play for over the next seven years.

In 2020, the average UK spend on AI deployment in large businesses (over 250 employees) was estimated to be £1.6m, with a further spend of £3.1m on labour associated with the development, operation or maintenance of AI. Forrester Research projected in 2021 that global custom AI software spend was expected to almost double from $33bn in 2021 to $64bn in 2025 and would grow 50% faster than the overall software market.

With such a diffuse landscape, it is a challenge for policymakers to identify how best to capitalise on data as a strategic national asset, when an estimated 75% of it is hidden away in proprietary silos in major global corporates. However, one thing that is startlingly obvious from all the research is that harnessing data innovation in these companies represents a huge opportunity for exponential growth in a data-driven economy.

Of course, a lot of the work to be done involves skills and developing data maturity within firms. The UK government's Invest 2035 industrial strategy green paper, published in October 2024, flags up the importance of 'improving data maturity in businesses to help businesses to do more with data – both as users and producers. This includes improving competition in data-driven markets, and collaborative government and private sector arrangements on consistent standards, data-sharing infrastructure, and supporting businesses in the way data is used across supply chains.'[26]

At my round tables and in interviews, senior leaders in these businesses told me they feel 'overlooked' in consultation processes because their opinions are seen as 'out of touch' and 'not as relevant' as those of technology providers. They have serious concerns around the impacts and applicability of new regulations (particularly regarding AI) in industrial, multi-jurisdictional and enterprise-scale environments.

Recommendations for UK policymakers

1. **The creation of an industry forum to advance the UK's applied AI opportunities.**
   Many business leaders in the UK I have spoken to have lamented the absence of a 'DeepTech Business Council' which could combine industry knowledge to safely accelerate

the real-world applications for AI and machine learning at-scale. This should be cross-economy and focused on the impacts on research and development in the UK's leading sectors, rather than on AI as a core technology.

Bringing together domain and technical experts from different market segments, the Council would act as interlocutor with government and regulators, while supporting both the world-class research of the UK's leading institutions and the work of the AI Safety Institute, both in advancing safe and secure core technologies, and supporting cross-sector collaboration, so the existing domain expertise, innovations and best-practice from different industries can be harnessed.

2. **Sectoral regulators should not be left to address AI regulation without close central coordination and input from industry. The government should bring together all sectoral and economic regulators to ensure an aligned approach on AI policy, development and regulation.**
   With the UK's current sectoral risk approach, which considers the domain-specific impact of core AI technologies, different regulators are responsible for aligning rulemaking, high-level goals and direction. By not considering the wider economic impacts of AI deployment at-scale, this is currently being done without coordinated input from enterprise-scale businesses, which are best-placed to release exponential value and create jobs, by deploying AI in industrial and service environments.

   As international standards around AI and ML safety and security are developed, we must look not just at the borderless core technologies, but also at where the real-world impacts will be felt, from job creation and value delivery, through to data and the residency of intellectual property.

The World Economic Forum has said that AI raises unprecedented challenges 'in relation to algorithmic accountability, data protection, explainability of decision-making by machine-learning models and potential job displacements'.[27] The companies I have spoken to are genuinely concerned that the rules of the road are already being decided by a group of 'experts' who have very a different set of needs and priorities to their own: namely, the biggest technology firms and the lobbying organisations that represent them.

AI as a strategic national asset

Global spending on artificial intelligence, including software, hardware and services for AI-centric systems, was expected to reach $154bn in 2023, an increase of 26.9% over the amount spent the year before, according to data cited earlier from IDC, which went on to point out: 'The Enterprise DataSphere will grow more than twice as fast as the Consumer DataSphere over the next five years, putting even more pressure on enterprise organisations to manage and protect the world's data while creating opportunities to activate data for business and societal benefits.'

The government's Office for AI estimated that UK business expenditure on AI technologies could increase from £16.7bn in 2020 to £127bn in 2040 – that's a rapidly growing pie for enterprise software providers. But it's a worthwhile investment if the technologies are going to deliver on their promises.

It has been several years since McKinsey projected that 'AI could potentially deliver additional economic output of around $13tn by 2030, boosting global GDP by about 1.2 percent a year',[28] and a lot has changed since, but the figure is still being quoted widely (such as in the 2023 Tony Blair Institute for Global Change report[29]) as the promise of significant value release across the economy is too good an opportunity to miss. In 2022, the Intellectual Property Office also reported: 'It has been estimated that by 2030, wider implementation of AI in the UK could result in a 22% boost to the UK economy.' More recently, in 2024,

McKinsey estimated that generative AI alone could add up to $4.4tn in value to the global economy.

The question which needs to be asked is, which companies, countries and people will be the ones to benefit from this rapid growth? AI is clearly a strategic asset, but for whom?

The 2019 *Government AI Readiness Index* (which ranks countries globally using 39 indicators across ten dimensions) found the UK was good at developing AI solutions but lacking in the wider scale adoption of them. However, the 2023 edition found that across its three pillars – government, technology sector and data & infrastructure – the UK ranked top in Western Europe, and third globally for AI readiness, behind the United States and Singapore.[30] The analysts at Oxford Insights, which produces the index, felt that recent developments, like strategic government investment and the Bletchley Declaration which emerged from the AI Safety Summit, have helped to improve the UK's position as a global hub for AI innovation.[31]

The UK is also currently number three in the world in both creation of unicorn ($1bn valuation) startups and as a destination for private investment in AI (behind the USA and China in both cases), but most of those valuations – 17 – are for finance technology (fintech) companies.[32] In addition to a deliberately innovation-friendly regulatory approach, the principal reason for this is the rigour with which financial markets in the UK are regulated, the idea being that if a fintech startup can make it here, they can make it anywhere.

Because AI is a general purpose technology, which can be applied in just about any data-rich environment, the same robust legislative environment and supportive ecosystems simply don't exist to support AI and ML growth, either for startups or corporate spin-outs, in the UK.

Over the last decade, the UK has developed one of the world's most supportive environments for tech startups and scale-ups, coalescing talent, funding, research, innovation and government support around a resilient but supportive regulatory regime.

While this has proven to be a successful foundation for nurturing talent and the UK has developed a global reputation for producing technology startups – particularly in fintech – this ecosystem hasn't reached the innovation happening in large companies in the same way it has with the micro, small and medium sized enterprise (SME) market and there now appears to be an associated lag in adoption of AI at-scale in the UK, compared to Europe and the USA.

Despite an environment which is generally supportive to innovation, the UK suffers from a lack of native investment in novel technologies: the AI business sector tends to be dominated by the multinational conglomerates. Similarly, the majority of high-volume patent assignees are based in the USA (Microsoft, Alphabet, IBM, Facebook, Yahoo, Intel, Amazon, Apple and Qualcomm), according to a research paper by Cowan & Hinton.[33]

A related challenge in the UK for many startups working on AI and machine learning technologies is the distinct lack of availability of relevant data on which to train foundation models, as stated in the IPO's 2022 report: 'Even if a unique AI technology or solution is developed, there may be a lack of suitable training data available in the UK.'

The corporate data held in-house by the largest businesses is fiercely protected for competitive reasons, so it is incredibly challenging for innovators to access the problems they are designing solutions for. For many large corporates, the justifiable fear of sharing data is a huge incentive to acquire startups, rather than running the risk of collaborating with them. As the report finds, 'Large companies have a potential monopoly on main data resources.'

This was also indicated in the *Corporate AI Capabilities* survey, where I found that enterprise firms are four times more likely to outsource or buy-in AI products from third party providers than to collaborate with partners to co-create AI/ML products.

Yet there is an appetite among the tech leaders in these companies to collaborate more widely. The CTO in a large electrical conglomerate told me: 'I'd love to collaborate, but the NDAs take longer than the projects!'

The *Barriers to Digital Transformation* survey showed that CIOs, CTOs and AI Directors see the most value in collaborating with other companies facing into similar transformation challenges. However, competitive instincts mean these are the least likely collaborations for their businesses to pursue, preferring instead to work with government agencies and academia.

Where 1 is least useful and 5 is most useful, please rank how useful it would be for your company to collaborate with...

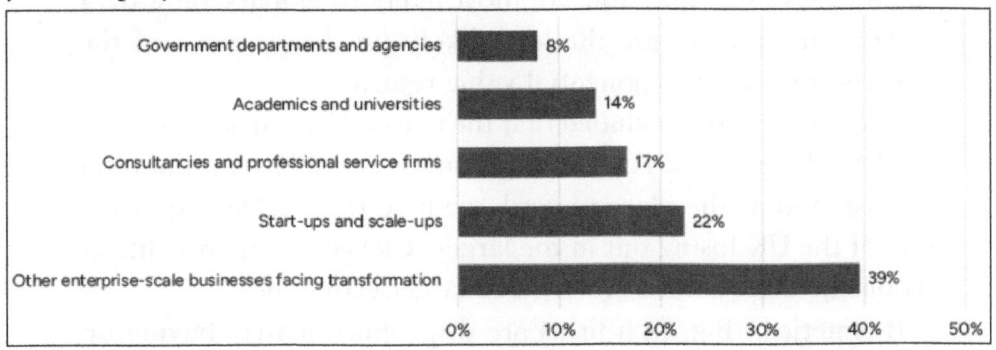

Firstly, technology leaders were asked to rank how useful it would be for their companies to collaborate – sharing knowledge, data and/or experience – with a range of potential partners. Secondly, they were asked which of these their company was most or least likely to collaborate with.

Where 1 is least likely and 5 is most likely, please rank which your company is most or least likely to collaborate with...

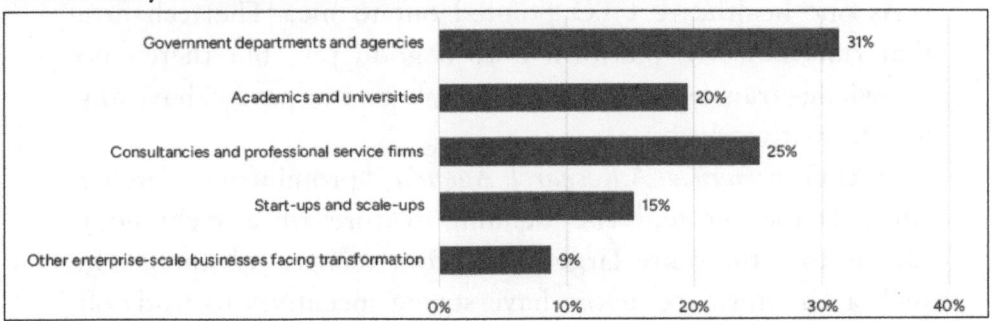

What is immediately telling about these two charts is that senior tech leaders would really value the chance to work closely with other businesses facing the same challenges, but – based on anecdotal insights from the interviews – don't feel they can collaborate with other companies which have enough resources to 'steal their supper'.

Instead, their companies are far more likely to collaborate with government departments and agencies, which the tech leaders feel would be the least useful collaboration for them to undertake. What the charts actually show is that the partners the businesses in question are most likely to embark on a data collaboration with, are the least likely (in the opinions of the experts) to deliver exponential value return.

The IPO report concluded that the reason UK startups move to the USA because: 'It is a far larger market and has a reputation for risk and as the place to get large investment. This poses the risk of the UK losing out in the larger-scale economic benefits of AI business growth to other much larger economies.'

If American Big Tech firms are disproportionately buying up innovation, offshoring intellectual property, helping to design the playing field, influencing policy and vacuuming up talent, how difficult will it be for the biggest companies, who arguably have the most at stake, to capitalise on the opportunities AI and machine learning offers, without outsourcing their solutions to an enterprise provider? And what are the dependency risks of failing to hire and develop the talent needed to build technology in-house?

As one healthcare CTO pointed out to me, 'The tech firm that runs our ML platform does a good job, but there's no knowledge transfer and very few people on our payroll have any idea how it works.'

In *AI Governance: A Research Agenda*,[34] prominent researcher Allen Defoe wrote, 'The defining feature of a technology race is that there are large gains from relative advantage. In such a circumstance actors have strong incentives to trade-off against other values (like safety, transparency, accountability, democracy) and opportunities, in order to increase the probability of gaining advantage. In particular, a worry is that it may be close to a necessary and sufficient condition for AI safety and alignment that there be a high degree of caution prior to deploying advanced powerful systems; however, if actors are competing in a domain with large returns to first-movers or relative advantage, then they will be pressured to choose a sub-optimal level of caution.'

We are in a situation where the Big Tech players highlighted in the previous chapter have a disproportionate role in advising governments and policymakers while competing for that relative advantage, and old-school corporations who have already quietly invested billions in tech development (and the laggards, who have yet to embark on the same journey) may have little choice but to conform to a set of guardrails and guidelines which have been, in part, designed by the companies who stand to benefit the most from selling them solutions.

Academic Andrew Rogoyski, from the Institute for People-Centred AI, says: 'I have grave concerns that governments have ceded leadership in AI to the private sector, probably irrecoverably. It's such a powerful technology, with great potential for good and ill, that it needs independent oversight that will represent people, economies and societies which will be impacted by AI in the future.'

This lack of input from industrial organisations is a two-way street: while policymakers don't actively court their opinion, most industry and technology leaders I spoke to don't have the time or inclination to be more actively involved in contributing to government tech policy or AI regulation. But it is important to keep them informed about developments, so they can future-proof their businesses against disruption and build more informed and sustainable data strategies.

As the *AI Readiness Index* pointed out, the UK is well positioned to take a global leadership role in the development of artificial intelligence. But several key components are missing for this to become a reality:

- Increasing access to supercompute capability;
- Improving the digital skills agenda (from school-age to the workforce);
- Ringfencing competitive pay for technical talent;
- Encouraging large corporates to patent their in-house technology;
- Making it easier for UK firms to acquire or invest in UK startups;
- Providing both technical and domain experts a seat at the table.

6

Bridging the
AI capability gap

Conducted through an online survey and qualitative interviews between 1 August and 15 September 2023, the *Corporate AI Capabilities* benchmarking survey captured the views of more than 100 of the UK's biggest businesses.

While the other research featured in this book focused on digital transformation, culture and the growing dependency senior executives have on data, this is was the first in-depth look at how prepared enterprise-scale businesses are to unlock economic value from data-driven technologies.

The country's 400 largest companies, most of which are older than the internet, employ 15.2m people – 8.1m in the UK (26% of the workforce). Their data, much of which is hidden in proprietary silos, is notoriously difficult to access and hard to extract value from.

Most companies don't reveal their spend on novel technologies, but this survey painted the first clear picture about large UK firms' data strategies, levels of expertise at the top and how important they think AI will be for them in the next few years.

As any good Chief Data Officer will tell you, you always need to be aware of the biases and prejudices you bring to data analytics. Only when I started digging into the combined data from 91 survey respondents and 26 interviewees – and failed to find what I was looking for – did I see how sage that advice is.

So, what did I expect to find? From qualitative interviews, I got the impression that AI capabilities would be easy to map against market segments: manufacturing, engineering, pharmaceutical and automotive firms seemed to be way ahead of consumer goods, mining and professional services businesses.

And that is true for some, but wildly false for others. What the research actually illustrated was that when looking at respondents who had been actively using AI, machine learning and data science for 'less than two years', 'between two and five years', 'more than five years', or 'not at all', the respondents came from businesses across all market segments. Regardless of sector, businesses in each of these 'age groups' had a huge amount in common.

Survey respondents across all sectors were asked to compare both their own current level of investment in data-driven technologies and their technical capabilities in AI, ML and data science with their direct competitors. From the research, there emerged a set of correlations between business size, current (and future) levels of investment, willingness to collaborate with external partners and their levels of data literacy at executive levels. The results made it relatively easy to categorise all the firms that took part as being in one of what I have called the four stages of AI maturity.

The four stages of AI maturity

AI newbies

'We can't find AI suppliers that will do what we need for the budget we have available. We can't even get our loyalty app to work consistently.'

CIO, Hospitality

There were 11 companies in the sample where respondents reported they didn't use AI or machine learning at all, had no data strategy in place and had no senior executives with technology backgrounds or experience.

The one obvious caveat here is that survey responses always reflect a subjective moment in time and it may be that the respondents were not aware of AI activity in their businesses. However, all bar one of the AI newbies self-identified as a member of top management in their businesses, so one must assume a level of informed representation.

The most common challenge among this group was not really knowing how to get started on their AI journey and the most common fear was that their business would be left behind by more capable competitors.

While still enterprise-scale, AI newbies had the smallest headcounts in the survey (averaging 4,600 UK full-time employees (FTE)) and they were most likely to be in the hospitality, food and beverage, chemical engineering or legal sectors.

Gifted youngsters

'I need to explain that good ML investments don't yield immediate business value in the next quarter, but for the next ten quarters.'

CTO, Consumer goods

Twenty-seven companies in this group said they had been using AI or machine learning for less than two years and executive team respondents seemed quite concerned about the level of investment required to make AI work for them: both that they had spent an unprecedented amount already, and also that they recognised they needed to spend a lot more in the coming years, while feeling impatient – and perhaps a little nervous – about demonstrating the value return on their investments.

Gifted youngsters had a mean average business size of 10,000 UK FTE and these firms were most likely to be making and selling consumer goods, or in the legal and professional services sectors.

Talented teens

'There is genuine fear of reputational risk at board level, which prevents us from implementing some technology that could be game-changing.'

AI Director, Defence

These 27 companies seem to be well on their way to AI success, having been actively using AI and machine learning for between two and five years. They generally felt they were only slightly ahead of the competition in terms of spend, but that they were comfortably ahead in terms of capability.

Their concerns at board and executive level were around guardrails and reputational risk – cautiously investing in capability while often waiting for the other shoe to drop. Talented teens from our survey averaged 17,750 UK FTE and were most likely to be in banking and financial services, as well as the defence and pharmaceutical sectors.

Promising adults

'The company is so large and the culture so siloed that it is hard to deploy new tech across multiple divisions, even if it would massively increase the value release.'

VP, Technology, Manufacturing

The final 26 businesses in the sample tended to be the largest (including all of the companies in the respondent pool with over

50,000 FTE in their UK entities, and around half of those with more than 25,000 FTE) and had been using AI for the longest, more than five years. This maturity showed at the top, as this was the cohort with the most executives and board members with technology experience or backgrounds.

More than three quarters of the promising adults had AI experts in senior management roles and almost half of them had a strategic data science lab or unit. Their biggest concerns were around their ability to deploy new technology at scale, across different departments or geographies, and trying to create the right digital culture.

Do you feel your management information (MI) has become more complex over the last three years?

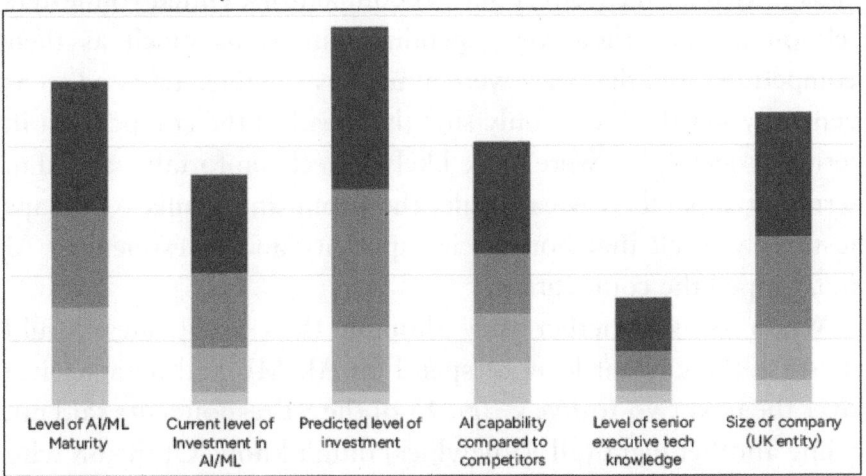

This chart shows a correlation between the size of a company, the number of years they had been using AI, their current AI investment and their predicted level of spend over the next two-to-five years.

Two things jump out of this chart: firstly that the talented teens and promising adults are the most likely to predict an increase in AI investment over the next few years; the second is that regardless of size, the level of senior executive tech knowledge is generally perceived to be low across all stages of AI maturity. The presence of technology expertise or background among the senior executives and boards of the companies in question still correlated with AI maturity but perceptions were disproportionately lower than other metrics in all cohorts.

Investment in AI, ML and data science

On the subject of current and future investment in data-driven technologies, interviewees were keen to point out the difference between general purpose AI (like large language models, such as ChatGPT) and applied machine learning technology, which is purpose-built to solve some of their most complex problems.

AI newbies, unsurprisingly, felt they invested less and had lower capability than their direct market competitors. Gifted youngsters felt on average they were spending almost as much as their competitors and that they were almost as capable. Talented teens generally felt they were only slightly ahead of the competition in terms of spend, but were more likely to feel comfortably ahead in terms of capability. Meanwhile, the promising adults – perhaps justifiably – felt that both their capability and investment in AI outstripped the competition.

When asked whether they thought their companies would increase the current level of spend on AI, ML and data science over the next two-to-five years, 15 of the 91 respondents said no, while another eight (all AI newbies) didn't know. Of the 68 who did predict an increase, the bullishness of their expectations was in line with their AI maturity, but the majority predicted a future investment of up to 50% in the coming years.

Across the survey sample, 59% of business leaders said they believed their AI capability was lower than their direct competitors, while 58% did not have an AI expert in the top three tiers of management.

Most of the companies I spoke to don't want their competitors to know how much they spend on AI development and, because this is often done in-house, using proprietary data for commercial benefit or to find marginal (but extremely valuable) gains, there isn't a universal way to measure levels of investment.

Digging in to how major corporates prefer to build or procure their data-driven technologies, fewer than a quarter (24%) of respondents said they bought in ready-made products from third party providers, while over a third (39%) told us they outsourced some or all of their AI/ML development to third parties. Fewer than one in five (19%) said they already built products in-house.

Anecdotally, several interviewees – from companies in the 19% who build their products in-house – alluded to the possibility that they had already invested tens or even hundreds of millions of pounds on AI and machine learning capabilities, yet even the most experienced leaders felt their companies were at an early stage in their journeys.

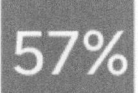

57%

of senior executives felt their company wasn't investing heavily in AI... however a third felt their company was investing heavily.

75%

of business leaders expected their firms to increase investment in AI, machine learning & data science over the next two years.

65%

of AI-mature enterprise firms would consider acquiring (or have already acquired) an AI/ML startup to enhance their capabilities.

More than half (57%) of senior executives felt their company wasn't spending as much on AI as their direct competitors... however, a third felt their company was investing more. Three quarters (75%) of business leaders expected their firms to increase investment in AI by 2028.

And 65% of AI-mature 'promising adults' would consider acquiring (or have already acquired) an AI or ML startup to enhance their capabilities. Very few firms in the other age cohorts are in a situation to even consider doing so.

Exploring the people capabilities in these organisations, the research found that just over a fifth (22%) of the least mature firms had no in-house AI, ML or data science capabilities, while just under a fifth of the most mature (17%) either had a strategic data science unit or a large AI team already in place. The majority of respondents – the remaining 61% – reported they either had a small central AI team, or pockets of data science expertise dotted around the business.

Which statement(s) best describes your company's AI/ML/data science people capabilities?

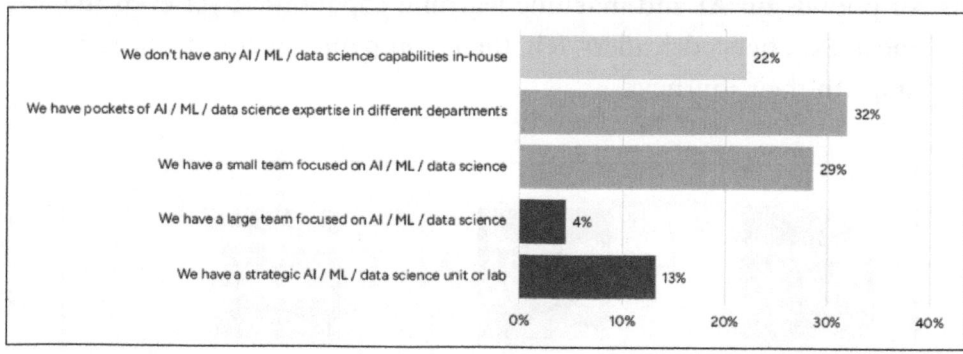

When it comes to collaboration, responses showed that enterprise-scale firms are four times more likely to outsource or buy-in AI products from third party providers than to collaborate with partners to co-create them. Promising adults were the most likely to work with partners, followed by talented teens and then gifted youngsters. Five of the gifted youngsters and all 11 AI newbies said they didn't buy or build any AI products at all, which may demonstrate a lack of awareness of where artificial intelligence applications are already embedded into products they already use.

Executive data literacy

The relatively sudden arrival on the scene of user-friendly and popular generative AI platforms from OpenAI and a number of other firms created a tidal wave of media coverage, which prompted a greater level of interest at board-level than any technology that has gone before it in recent years. Businesses of all sizes have spent considerable time in the last few years trying to work out what generative AI might be able to do for them, what efficiencies might be found and how productivity might be able to increase. Accenture found that 95% of global executives believe next-generation computing will be a major driver of breakthroughs in their industry over the next decade.[1]

This board-level interest has added pressure to act for many businesses, though not always in the most strategic ways. As one pharmaceutical CIO told me, 'We need a better data strategy. The AI part isn't the biggest obstacle, it's getting people to adopt so we can operate at scale.' This is true even in digitally mature businesses where artificial intelligence and machine learning are already well entrenched in the organisation. A medical device CTO told me, 'We have used AI to optimise our factories, our workforce and our supply chain. Now, the CEO wants us to "just use AI to generate more revenue". Like it's that simple!'

Lack of senior executive and board understanding of the value of data is holding many pioneers back from instituting transformational change. The *Disruption Index* report from consulting firm Alix Partners found that 83% of large corporate CEOs say their board of directors impedes the process of adopting essential new technology solutions.[2] The same survey found that 85% of CEOs say it has become increasingly difficult to know what to prioritise themselves. Discussing these findings with our interviewees, a manufacturing CTO told me, 'The hard part begins after the proof of concept. Senior executives whose teams would benefit most from a rollout refuse to sponsor because they simply don't understand the value and don't want the disruption.'

Several of the tech leaders I spoke to agreed that discussion of urgent technology deployment was often de-prioritised in meetings. Even when trying to commission outside expertise, an automotive data science VP said, 'Onboarding an AI partner and going through the whole RFP process is a nightmare without executive buy-in. There's no way I can onboard a supplier in less than three months because the C-suite don't understand the urgency.'

Interviewees consistently told me that business leaders struggle to make informed decisions around data strategy. It showed up in the data: respondents estimated that only 9.01% of management executives and fewer than one in 25 (3.74%) of board members have any background or experience in technology.

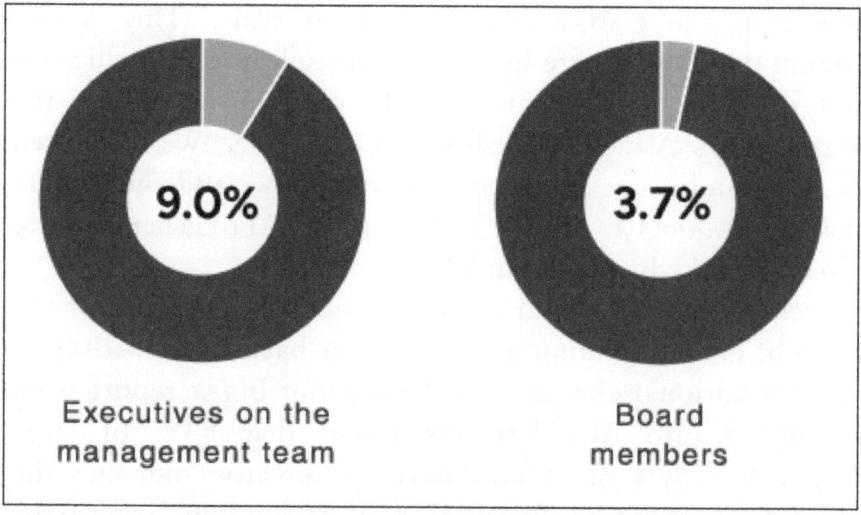

Businesses with tech expertise on both Exco and board were more likely to be found in automotive, transport and logistics sectors (50% of our sample), while banking and finance had the greatest proportion (71%) of firms with a technology seat at the management table (if not on the board).

There was a correlation between how long companies have been working with AI and ML, and an increase in tech knowledge at the top, with promising adults way ahead of the rest of the groups, averaging 17.69% of senior executives and 7.69% of board members with technology backgrounds or experience.

Tech experience at executive & Board level

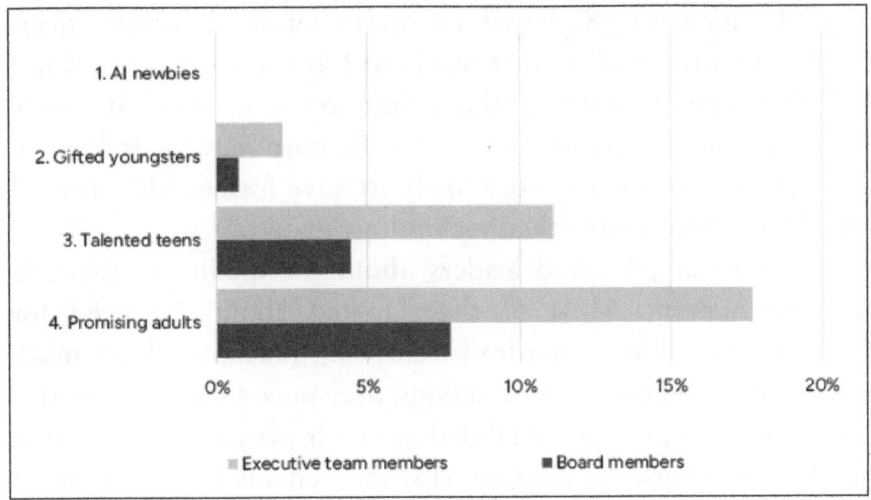

When asked which job level most closely described their company's most senior AI, ML or data science expert, only four respondents said it was someone on the executive team. All four were promising adults... and three of those were CTOs or CDIOs describing themselves.

'None of the above' was selected by all the AI newbies, the majority (89%) of gifted youngsters, nearly half (44%) of talented teens and just under a quarter (23%) of promising adults. Across the survey, close to six in ten (58%) said they didn't have an AI expert in the top three tiers of management.

The sectors most likely to employ a senior data scientist were banking, financial services, mining, automotive, aerospace, logistics and heavy manufacturing. Banking and financial services was the market segment which had the highest occurrence of AI experts at 'Leader/Head of (CEO-3)' levels.

With new regulations filtering through in most jurisdictions and the size of the AI market predicted to more than quadruple by 2030, these companies will be more dependent than ever on data to make decisions. Yet 91% of executive team members are believed to lack technology experience and only 42% of firms have an AI expert in the top three tiers of management.

(Interestingly, EY's 2024 *Boardroom Monitor* report found that the majority (82%) of European financial services firms (91% of banks) had at least one board director with experience of either a ministerial or parliamentary position or a civil service or government-appointed role.[3] So big corporates – at least in financial services – are more likely to have former MPs around their boardroom table than technology experts!)

In interviews, I asked leaders about the quality of their AI decision-making. Most of them talked about the need for 'human-in-the-loop' guardrails: ensuring machines don't mark their own homework when making decisions. One question this research raises, is: how qualified are your people to make good quality decisions? Would you trust the humans in your loop?

Bridging the AI capability gap is an urgent business need. Demand for experienced data strategists far outstrips supply, so it isn't possible to fix the problem by simply hiring more experts: we need a fresh approach to improving data literacy at all levels and we need to upskill current and future leaders, now.

Pattern recognition: sectoral highlights from the qualitative interviews

Most **automotive** businesses I interviewed are still in the process of moving from older legacy systems onto cloud-based platforms like Microsoft Azure and combining this with AI, Business Intelligence (BI) and visualisation tools like Tableau. Implementing AI is a slow work in progress, with a lack of understanding of precisely how it will add value to their firms, but the aim is to utilise more AI going forward. The CIOs I spoke to identified poor data literacy at all levels in their businesses, saying they struggled to communicate the value of the data that they manage. Automotive firms tend to cling to old-world processes, which need to be refined before automation, artificial intelligence or machine learning can be deployed.

'One of the biggest problems for all organisations is data literacy. Nobody in their operation understands the validity and implication of the data they are managing.'

VP Data Science, Automotive

'Even department heads and executives don't understand what [data literacy] means at an organisational level. They need to understand the value of the data they manage.'

CIO, Automotive

Medical devices & healthcare firms I spoke to tended to have been early adopters of AI-driven processes; however, their implementation and usage is still facing obstacles, mostly concerning enterprise-wide distrust of AI capabilities and security. Interviewees expressed frustration at knowledge gaps, particularly from their senior legal, regulatory, operations and compliance colleagues around the ability to share and utilise data. Constantly evolving legislation differs between regions of the world, often hampering full scale roll-out of AI solutions across companies in this segment. Fine tuning is needed to make AI use more efficient and wide-reaching, but the priority for these technology leaders is enhancing knowledge, learning, techniques and experience, especially at senior levels.

'AI processes need a lot of fine tuning to make them really deliver value. It's a question of applying experience, knowledge and using the right learning techniques to train the team to use them.'

CTO, Medical Devices

'Once you've decided how to capture data, you must ask yourself if you actually have the tools, the talent and capabilities to interrogate and make use of it. Most probably don't.'

CIO, Healthcare

'Embedding a digital mindset has been essential in applying a strategy and aligning our technology usage across four divisions.'

CIO, Medical Devices

'We could potentially diminish human errors, the overall error rate and increase accuracy. This could in turn reduce headcount costs in some areas. But the CEO keeps putting it off until next quarter, because he doesn't really get it.'

CIO, Healthcare

Pharmaceutical corporations have a big appetite to get more involved in using AI but face difficulties getting buy-in from senior directors, as they need to create a use-case for each AI project before obtaining executive or board buy-in. Friction caused by a lack of understanding in the operations and procurement teams also slows onboarding processes of new AI partners, further hampering AI deployment. One interviewee identified a growing appetite among senior executives to invest in Digital Twins as the digital health of patients has received a lot of coverage in the last couple of years, but this appetite seems to come from a place of satisfying shareholders, rather than understanding the inherent value of the technology.

'I know the company could achieve a lot of value if I could plug them into our way of thinking. But I've realised the demand signal needs to come from the CEO or CFO who can then engage the company and make sure it is executed.'

CIO, Pharmaceutical

'We have invested a lot in the right tools, but have had to outsource the skills to run them. It's extremely hard to build the skills in-house, and it isn't sustainable.'

CTO, Pharmaceutical

'We learned the importance of having a cohesive team with the same digital vocabulary so they can both communicate data strategy and engineering, to deliver value back into the business.'

VP Digital, Pharmaceutical

Precision engineering and tooling businesses tend to use specific AI and ML programmes widely, particularly across supply chain and procurement areas. Leaders I interviewed reported that the value of AI in making marginal cost-savings at scale was widely recognised by their executive teams, but that it was difficult to communicate the value of data science in other areas of the businesses. They identified the need to 'upgrade' the digital skills of staff to really unlock value.

'AI is a 100% perfect fit for us. But training people will be imperative for AI success.'

CTO, Precision Engineering

'We do have a process in place to upskill our people to reach our goals. But without serious data science expertise and mentoring, it's going to take a lot longer to reach them. We need to ensure we upskill our trusted staff so they can work alongside the implementation of tech, so we achieve the right balance between human knowledge, experience and tech usage.'

CIO, Precision Tooling

Rail companies have complicated manufacturing processes and they are relatively new to implementing ML and AI solutions, usually in a phased approach, such as measuring decay in the train wagons and engines. The leaders I spoke to have realised some value from AI in predictive repair and contract negotiation, but data science is not widely used or understood across their businesses. There is no need to use data science for procurement or supplier selection, as they tend to use few and long-term partners as suppliers. One rail CIO was in the process of building an in-house AI lab, but recognised it was an experiment which needed to demonstrate results fast for the board to allow it to continue.

> 'The more we venture into new tech, the more we need to pay attention to the teams and processes. We have to constantly ensure our people are gaining the right skills.'
>
> CIO, Rail

> 'People are so resistant to change that even hated legacy systems are preferable to something new, intuitive and powerful, if they aren't open to understanding the value it can bring to their roles and the business.'
>
> CIO, Rail

Shipping and logistics businesses I spoke to were very advanced in terms of their internal data science structure and recognising where they could achieve the best impact with ML and AI. Data science is seen as essential, as small changes in a single route can cause delays elsewhere and have wide-ranging impacts across a network. Although they had clear plans for how they wanted to use AI, technology leaders in this segment had the opposite problem to other sectors in the digital skills space: there is an assumption that AI can fix everything and because it is already so embedded in business processes, executive colleagues confidently sign off on expensive AI projects, in service of marginal gains, without understanding the cost/benefit. This can cause a conflict between data science enthusiasm and meeting business objectives.

'Senior executives tend to be unclear on use cases. We have access to a huge amount of data, but few people understand where the nuggets of quality are hiding.'

Director of AI, Shipping

'We operate a high volume, narrow margin business. The cost of implementing new models and platforms can be prohibitive, but will fail without the right skills in-house to make them work.'

CTO, Logistics

'Investing in data literacy and culture at all levels during the pandemic was by far the most important step in creating a culture where new technologies can embed and deliver value.'

CIO, Shipping

Manufacturing firms I spoke to showed a great deal of AI maturity, with advanced machine learning deployments already well established. Many of the leaders were currently focused on using the technology to rationalise and optimise incredibly complex supply chains, to help meet their Net Zero commitments. One consistent challenge for the people I interviewed was around how to replicate AI successes across disparate geographies or departments with fundamentally different processes – sometimes in place for decades. The other was the never-ending effort to embed digital mindset and data innovation behaviours with any kind of consistency across large and distributed workforces.

'Our biggest learning was that we can't buy an "out-of-the-box" solution. For AI tools to deploy successfully, we need to work with the people who will use it. Those people need a digital mindset to co-create the technology.'

Group Head of AI, Manufacturing

'Every department now has digital ambassadors, every team has access to upskilling opportunities and every new starter is offered digital skills as part of their onboarding, regardless of where they work in the business.'

CIO, Manufacturing

'My colleagues all want to "use AI" but have next to no idea of where to start, what it involves, or how it will help them reach their business objectives.'

CTO, Manufacturing

7

Unlocking industrial value from AI and machine learning

The rate at which AI development will accelerate with the rise of quantum computing's increased processing capabilities is expected to be exponentially faster than ever before. As Hartmut Neven, founder of Google's Quantum AI lab, put it: 'It looks like nothing is happening, nothing is happening, and then whoops, suddenly you're in a different world.'

The *AI Activity in the UK* report noted higher levels of AI investment in some sectors (such as telecoms and legal) and lower in others (construction and hospitality). My research supports that trend. It is also possible to see correlations between an increase in technology R&D spend and a prevalence of complex industrial processes and/or heavily regulated environments – in other words, businesses that depend on consistency and measurability in output are more likely to invest in compute-powered assurance.

In its 2023 report on *The Economic Potential of Generative AI*,[1] McKinsey & Company wrote that, 'The midpoint scenario at which automation adoption could reach 50 percent of time spent on current work activities has accelerated by a decade.' Notably, the arrival of new gen-AI products from OpenAI and others has overturned earlier assumptions that automation would mostly impact low-wage, low-skill workers. 'Generative AI is likely to have the biggest impact on knowledge work, particularly activities involving decision making and collaboration, which previously had the lowest potential for automation,' says the report.

The 2023 KPMG *Global Tech Report* found that 57% of leaders believed that AI and machine learning, including generative AI, will be important in helping them achieve their business objectives over the following three years and 29% of businesses said they had seen a profitability or performance gain of at least 11% from investments in data analytics.

However, as was clear from my interviews, as well as the free text responses in the surveys, a lot of business leaders see AI and machine learning as 'just another' tool to help them reach their business goals. For some, wider adoption of data-driven technologies is fairly low on their priority lists, especially when compared to compliance or product safety.

While most of the companies I spoke to don't want their competitors to know how much they spend on AI development, in each of the ten market segments outlined in Chapter 4, it was possible to identify at least one (but often more) major global corporates whose investments in AI and machine learning capabilities were already in the tens (or hundreds) of millions. Three quarters of the leaders surveyed expect to increase investment over the next few years and most felt they were still early in their journeys, regardless of their level of AI maturity.

One message that was clear was that continuous education is a precondition for:

- changing mindset and behaviours
- increasing data quality
- improving data integrity

- assessing current organisational capability
- engaging executive sponsors in areas relevant for them
- communicating effectively

These are some of the key points that underpin the Data Success Framework which is outlined in Part Three.

Collaborative interventions: could companies achieve more together?

Because of the global nature of their businesses, the organisations that took part in the research own the world's largest and most complicated data sets and are likely to be the most impacted by regulatory change in multiple jurisdictions. They hold personal, business, sensitive and behavioural data on millions of customers worldwide. Each one is the custodian of billions of proprietary data points, hidden in silos – disparate systems, geographies and departments – which are difficult to analyse, interpret and unlock value from. Many of their systems have been designed with collection of data in mind, but no clear objectives on why the business would need it, so interrogating the many and varied sources of data is incredibly hard.

Harnessing data innovation in these companies represents a huge opportunity for exponential growth in a data-driven economy. However, news and policy about emerging technologies are often inaccessible and hard to understand, even for people with technical expertise, let alone for the 91% of executives and 96% of board members who my research suggests have no tech background.

One of the recurring themes in the conversations with CEOs and board members has been a sense of frustration from leaders with what one interviewee called 'silly AI media hype and technobabble'. They just want to know *how*, *when* and *why* technology will impact their people, their processes and their bottom lines.

The *Barriers to Digital Transformation* study showed that 39% of CIOs, CTOs and AI Directors saw the most potential value in collaborating with other companies facing similar transformation challenges. More than one in five (22%) were also keen to work with startups and scale-ups. However, competitive instincts embedded in these companies' DNA mean these are the least likely collaborations for their businesses to pursue.

Just over three-quarters (76%) of respondents to that survey said their companies were more likely to consider collaborations with government agencies, universities or management consultancies, than they were with other corporates on a similar data transformation journey, or with startups working with new technologies.

The CTOs I spoke to and the companies they work for have become exceptionally talented at finding targeted solutions to targeted problems. But system-wide problems require system-wide solutions and none of us can tackle massive challenges like sustainability, reducing carbon emissions and climate change alone.

Collaboration could be exactly the secret sauce needed for these organisations to be able to solve the big societal problems like the race to Net Zero, human trafficking, diversity, equity and inclusion, and yes, even digital transformation. Early discussions with both technical and operational leaders have shown there is a willingness to explore collaborations – especially with companies who do not directly compete in the same sectors.

There is a growing recognition – certainly among tech leaders, who tend to be more sector-agnostic than their domain specialist peers on the Exco – that large enterprises have far more in common than might be immediately obvious. As one retail CDO told me, 'We share the same problems alongside all enterprises of our scale. I've worked in banking: same problem. I've worked in media: same problem.'

The war for talent

The McKinsey Global Institute projections of the correlation between impacts of automation and skill levels showed that generative AI may actually level the playing field for knowledge workers. Clifford Chance found in its 2022 *Defining Tomorrow's Legal Function Through Its Relationships* report: 'Effective use of artificial intelligence for predictive purposes is seen as desirable but aspirational by most of the participants... There is consensus among participants that the technology is not yet sophisticated enough to have a big impact.'

At the World Economic Forum at Davos in 2024, AI was high on the agenda. Salesforce AI's Clara Shih said of herself and other CEOs, 'Every single one of us will need to write a new job description', while Paul Knopp, the US CEO at KPMG, said, 'We're at a phase where in 2024 we think generative AI will move from pilots and experiments to implementation and industrialisation'.

There is huge speculation on what impact the growing importance of generative AI will have on workforces. A 2023 Pew Research Center report suggests that 19% of American workers have a job with 'high exposure' to artificial intelligence,[2] which correlates with separate research published the same week by McKinsey,[3] which found that low wage earners are up to 14 times more likely to need to change occupations by 2030 than the highest earners.

Away from the headlines, the senior leaders I have spoken to have little to no expectation that AI will replace workers. Their firm hope (if not yet belief) is that AI will enable their workers to increase outputs, and to reduce variability in those outputs. Leaders recognise their employees are collaborators in a technology-enabled future. As one manufacturing CDO put it: 'For new tools to deploy successfully, we need to work with the people who will use them. Those people need a digital mindset to co-create the technology.'

While it was clear from the research that quite a few of the UK's biggest companies are already using artificial intelligence and other emerging technologies to solve complex DeepTech problems, many more are at much earlier stages on their data transformation journeys. As they grow in AI maturity, they will need to protect their productivity, their people and their profits. With the majority of them predicting an increase in investment over the next few years, AI's importance will only increase.

There is a broader and more nuanced discussion to be had around the importance of digital workforce skills and nurturing expert talent. The 2023 report from Future Dot Now showed that 59% of the UK workforce cannot complete all the digital tasks essential for work, but that 82% of jobs now require digital skills.[4] Recruitment of data science specialisms is on the rise: recruitment platform Indeed says the number of AI-related job postings increased from 20 to 328 per million between 2018 and 2023. Gartner estimated that, while only a quarter of Fortune 2000 companies had dedicated AI leadership at VP level or above in 2023, this was expected to increase to 80% imminently.

The future of work has been an evolving discussion since Covid. The employer–employee relationship (especially in the knowledge economy) has changed forever. With challenges around skills, migration and the seeming fungibility of the Gen-Z workforce, attracting and retaining talent is hard work for every business, in every industry.

With that said, there is an acute concern among the business leaders I have spoken to, with regard to their ability to recruit and retain data scientists, data engineers, software engineers and technical domain specialists. Competition is high, as are the salary expectations. Companies for whom data analytics is not the core activity, but rather a business enabler, are struggling to keep up. They expend a disproportionate amount of energy on trying to differentiate their offering, to find ways to compete with Big Tech firms, who look great on a CV and tend to offer (at least) twice as much in wages, regardless of the technical disciplines required.

Access to talent is a common problem across all sectors. In the *Barriers to Digital Transformation* survey the majority (55%) of technology leaders had little or no confidence that their workforce had the necessary culture and skills to deliver on their company's digital strategy, while none of the respondents expressed full confidence.

With 0 representing no confidence and 5 representing full confidence, how confident are you that your workforce has the necessary culture and skills to deliver on your company's digital strategy?

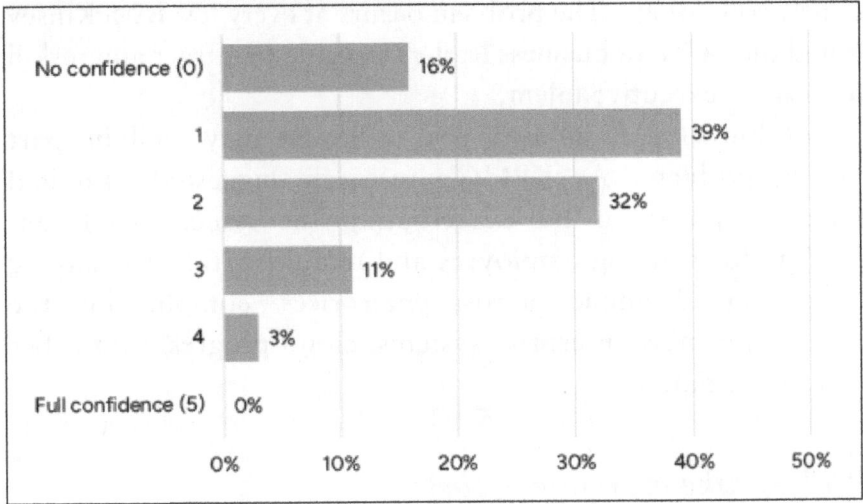

In the round tables and interviews, one issue that every single leader could agree on was the constant challenges around recruiting, retaining, training, upskilling and nurturing talent. Every major corporate trying to build its own data science team or develop AI and ML tools is competing with the brand cachet and much deeper pockets of US headquartered Big Tech firms.

Frank Bowley, who leads the UK government's Unit for Future Skills, said the Department for Education has developed a new skills taxonomy, breaking 3,000 or so job types across the economy into the requisite skills for a digitally enabled future, which should be helpful for employers in framing the capabilities their businesses will need moving forwards. Bowley said one of the most striking changes to the employment landscape in recent years has been that demand for empathy and coaching (behavioural skills) has risen faster than the demand for technical skills.

The *Disruption Index* reported that 'Finding enough employees with critical skills' was rated as the top workforce issue by 40% of CEOs, while in the 2022 *Global Tech Report*,[5] KPMG found that 44% of leaders cited 'Lack of capable talent (data scientists, engineers etc)' as their biggest challenge to adoption of new technology. The problem occurs at every level: McKinsey found that 47% of business leaders struggle to attract and reskill tech-savvy executive talent.

Not knowing how or where to invest may well be part of the problem. As KPMG's research suggested, 'Limited budgets appear to be exacerbating the issue. Insufficient funding for training employees and recruiting talent is having a widespread impact across enterprises, complicating the adoption of new enterprise systems, cloud progress and cyber security initiatives.'

Will AI take everyone's jobs?

The poll from Ipsos found that just 12% of over 5,000 UK adults polled believed AI would create more new job opportunities than the jobs that would be lost. 'Shifts in workflows triggered by these advances could expose the equivalent of 300 million full-time jobs to automation,' said analysts at Goldman Sachs,[6] predicting that AI could cause the partial automation of two-thirds of occupations over time. 'As tools using advances in natural language processing work their way into businesses and society, they could drive a 7% (or almost $7tn) increase in global GDP and lift productivity growth by 1.5 percentage points over a 10-year period.'

Meanwhile, research by tech consulting firm Cognizant predicted that generative AI is expected to significantly change

52% of all jobs, particularly those involving higher levels of knowledge work, by 2032.[7] These projections suggest that 9% of the workforce could be displaced, but only 1% of workers are likely to face challenges in finding new employment.

The rise in AI job displacement comes at a time of significant workplace change, thanks to the effects of the pandemic. Referring specifically to the employment market in America, Adam Posen, president of the Peterson Institute for International Economics, said, 'The enormous labour market churn of Covid in 2020–21 had the unintended benefit of moving millions of lower income workers to better jobs, more income security, and/ or running their own businesses.'

This isn't the first time in recent history that people have worried that technology would eliminate their job prospects. Karl T. Compton penned an essay about the 'Bogey of Technological Unemployment' in 1938, in the wake of the Great Depression, when one in five people in America were unemployed. The ones who weren't, were deeply concerned about the way new-fangled machinery was transforming farms, factories and industrial workplaces.

World War II meant there was no shortage of job opportunities, but the spectre loomed again in the early 1960s. In 1962, economist Robert Solow, who was awarded the 1987 Nobel Prize for his work on the role of technology in economic growth, noted that productivity in the post-war years – despite enormous technological advancement – only increased by 3%. 'That's nothing to be sneezed at, but neither does it amount to a revolution,' he said, explaining that the absence of a boom in productivity meant there was no evidence of a second Industrial Revolution that 'threatens catastrophic unemployment'.

In the 1990s, as internet-enabled personal computers landed on every knowledge worker's desk and email began to replace the fax machine, many economists and occupational researchers predicted huge job losses as traditional office roles were expected to be phased out by the new operational efficiencies that technology offered. But the paradigm shift to a more digital world – and consequently a far more globalised workforce – created many new roles with digital skills, which mitigated the phase-out of old ones.

In the early 2010s, following the financial crash, organisational academics Brynjolfsson *et al* argued that technological change was destroying jobs faster than it was creating them. Four years later, in his final speech as President in January 2017, Barack Obama talked about 'The relentless pace of automation that makes a lot of good middle-class jobs obsolete'. But how much of that obsolescence was due to a sluggish global economy? This was during the 'austerity' years when countries like Britain and Germany focused huge resources on innovation as a facilitator of growth and job creation, so while robots and automation were eliminating many industrial jobs, it is worth noting that thousands of smaller startups appeared at the same time, creating new digital-first roles that had never existed before.

Looking to the current decade, the 400 old-world enterprise-scale businesses I keep referring to collectively employed nearly 600,000 more people in the UK in 2023 than they did ten years earlier, in 2013. They may well be fundamentally different roles, but these companies still gainfully employ an estimated 8.1m people in the UK alone.

In conversations with many business leaders about the economic impacts of AI, most hoped that AI-enabled productivity gains would keep them competitive and robust for the future. While technology becomes more proficient at traditionally human roles, there is a risk of workforce displacement, but they are all frantically trying to hire employees with digital skills. Even companies feeling the economic pinch and enforcing global hiring freezes are prepared to make exceptions for technical talent.

Tied to this is a demographic challenge that sees the 'boomer' generation racing towards retirement, while there are simply fewer people in the younger generations getting ready to step into their places. A lot of companies I have spoken to are partly dependent on recruiting technical talent based overseas or importing expertise through technology visa schemes. Leaders are concerned that, as many of the world's leading democracies have begun pursuing more isolationist policies (like Brexit) in the last few years, it is becoming increasingly difficult for talent to migrate, in order to pursue career opportunities.

This raises an interesting macroeconomic question for the next decade or so about whether the under-supply of skilled workers or the displacement of old-school labour will prove to cause the greatest impact. In a 2022 research paper,[8] David Autor *et al* calculated that 60% of employment in 2018 consisted of job roles that didn't exist in 1940. One of the key questions they raised was whether job 'automation is accelerating relative to augmentation, as many researchers and policymakers fear'.

'The skills required for every job will change,' said Katy George, chief people officer at McKinsey. The big question is whether, 'We just exacerbate some of the problems that we've seen with previous waves of automation, but now in the knowledge sector, as well.' On how it is likely to affect the humans in the loop, she went on to say, 'The concern is, even though on net it will be a positive for the workforce, and there's lots of opportunity, individuals will not feel that way.'

'AI will not replace humans, but the humans who use AI intelligently will replace those who don't,' says author Mo Gawdat, former chief business officer at Google X, in his book *Scary Smart*.[9]

Upskilling the current workforce

In companies which employ tens of thousands of people – sometimes including unionised workforces – salaries have a baked-in price sensitivity, especially when building advanced data tools is not the core business activity. In those incumbent, hierarchical organisations, it is problematic to create junior roles with senior salaries in order to compete, which makes it difficult to attract and retain digital talent in such a competitive environment.

Faced with this, most big businesses looking to build or maintain an AI practice have programmes in place to hire young and relatively inexpensive talent from a range of degrees and backgrounds, with the intention of training them up. In order for this to work, those companies also need to be able to attract and retain top-flight (expensive) technical experts in order to surround inexperienced talent with knowledgeable leadership and strong mentoring skills, as most newly qualified data scientists and engineers can appreciate the trade-off between a lower salary and the chance to learn on the job.

But the leaders I have spoken to say the strategy of investing time and resources into training new hires carries inherent flight risks. As one civil engineering CTO told me, 'Juniors with nine months' experience are approached every day on LinkedIn, being offered 100% pay increases to move to a company their friends have heard of. We offer the chance to solve really big, systemic problems, but they also have bills to pay.' Furthermore, if the senior experts are poached – or leave to launch their own startup – their teams tend to follow them anyway.

Gawdat offers a great illustration of AI-enabled knowledge work in the (near) future: 'There will still be a need for lawyers, for example. It's just that we'll need fewer of them – and they will be the ones able to draft, review and litigate a smart contract, using AI, instead of the long-winded written contracts of today. They will be more efficient than lawyers have ever been because they'll start delegating the complex parts to smart machines. The lawyers who don't develop the skills needed to keep up will probably descend to jobs that demand less intellectual work and get paid less as a result.'

It isn't just people who work in technology who need to be upskilled. Which is why it is so important to embed a digital mindset and data innovation across your employee population. Not only does it improve your organisation's resilience and chances of success in digital transformation programmes, but it helps to safeguard their careers in an uncertain future.

If you want to unlock value from artificial intelligence, machine learning and data science, you need to create an environment where it can not only survive, but thrive.

You need a data culture.

PART THREE

How to succeed with Data Culture

The Periodic Table of Data Strategy Elements

Digital mindset & data innovation behaviours

The cultural building blocks of data strategy

'There is no silver bullet for transformation,' said Zahra Bahrololoumi, UK and Ireland CEO at Salesforce. 'But what has been a common theme is the need for the right talent and the rotation of skills to be able to fuel and get the value from that transformation. If you focus on something like analytics, everyone wanted to pursue the analytic utopia and two out of three investments, I think, failed. It was not the technology, it was actually, "Were the right processes in place?", "Did the organisations have the right talent?", "Do you have the right sponsorship and governance?"'

This view is consistent with what interviewees and round table participants consistently reported throughout my research: that they can not realise the full return on investment from any enterprise-level data transformation project until they first create a culture where data innovation can flourish.

It also chimes with a great deal of academic study in the area of organisational transformation. In 2012, John Ward and Axel Uhl analysed lessons from 13 different case studies, arguing that change programmes, 'Must have a clear strategic rationale explained in a language which everyone can understand. Otherwise there will be little motivation to change.'[1]

A year later, Chris Bilton and Stephen Cummings said that, in order to encourage 'creative management', 'Organisations have to be loose enough to allow for new ideas and inputs to be released and thus regenerate them, whist at the same time being controlled enough to draw these diverse inputs into a common direction.' [2]

This push–pull friction is at the heart of understanding how to develop a digital mindset and data innovation behaviours in a business environment.

Backed up by decades of research from all over the world, the round table discussions and in-depth interviews I've conducted have confirmed the maxim that, 'Data culture is about crafting the right environment and fostering the right behaviours, practices and communities to leverage the benefits of data.'

Organisations – especially the enterprise-scale ones the research focused on – are complex and multi-faceted, facing often paradoxical and conflicting challenges when trying to harness, understand and realise value from the data they have at their disposal. Creating a comprehensive data strategy which can capture those challenges requires a maturity of approach that is rare, especially in old-world businesses which are mature in other ways, having existed for decades, or perhaps even hundreds of years.

Aspiration is easy, but action is far more difficult and takes time: there is no quick solution to organisational change. Embedding a digital mindset enables data adoption, which accelerates data maturity, which is why I have worked with over a dozen domain experts, transformation directors and senior technology executives to discuss, test and develop the Periodic Table of Data Strategy Elements. With its foundations originating from a novel innovation framework conceived by Cerestiral LLP's co-founder and transformation expert Manisha Mistry, whose pioneering work was used to upskill over 50,000 people in digital skills during the pandemic, the periodic table has been developed with scalability and common challenges in mind, with a view to being able to roll it out in almost any business or industry.

When the objective is as complex as building a data strategy, we need to start at the end and work our way back...

For a leadership team to build a cohesive data strategy which truly unlocks value from technology, they must fully understand the sources of their organisation's data and establish interoperability between the input systems, channels and interfaces they use to gather that data, across different silos.

However, before they can do this effectively, they must first come to understand data as a strategic asset, which – like any asset – needs to be nurtured, developed and grown.

In order to achieve these things, the humans in the business first need to adopt a digital mindset and develop data innovation behaviours. These two combined will form a data culture where innovation can thrive and where data strategy can flourish.

As illustrated on the following page, the Periodic Table of Data Strategy Elements divides into two sub-groups: **Data Culture**, comprised of the mindset and behavioural (human) elements required to embrace new ways of working; and **Data Strategy**, comprised of the organisational (corporate) considerations which are necessary for businesses to design those new ways of working.

Data Culture vs. Data Strategy

'Culture eats strategy for breakfast', a quote apocryphally credited to management consultant Peter Drucker, is a favoured mantra in business school lore. To stretch the breakfast analogy, I would say that if strategy is the meal, then culture is everything the chef needs to serve it, from the ingredients to the saucepan, the oven to the whisk – culture is the whole kitchen!

What you may notice from this table is that more than half of the elements I identified to unlock growth are about building a

The Periodic Table of Data Strategy Elements

Data Culture

Developing a Digital Mindset

1 Embracing The Unknown	2 Openness, Flexibility & Adaptability	3 Humility & EQ	4 Entrepreneurship	5 Design Thinking	6 Diversity, Equity & Inclusion	7 Agile and Lean Methodology	8 Thinking Like A Start-up	9 Experimentation
10 Risk Awareness	11 Data Literacy	12 Lifelong Learning	13 Fostering Collaboration	14 Building Networks & Communities	15 Exploring Possibility Together	16 Sharing Ideas & Good Practices	17 Engaging & Empowering	18 Using Data to Drive Decision Making

Embedding Data Innovation Behaviours

19 Being Braver & Bolder	20 Becoming Pioneers Together	21 Being Responsive to New Information	22 Embracing Positive Disruption	23 Taking Risks	24 Failing Fast	25 Learning Through Feedback Loops	26 Iterating Better Solutions

Data Strategy

Understanding Data as a Strategic Asset

27 Data Quality & Hygiene	28 Data Integrity	29 Data Ethics	30 Cyber Security & Resilience	31 Data Engineering & Architecture	32 Programming and Software Inputs	33 Data Governance	34 Internal & External User Experience	35 Data Science & Innovation
36 ML, Analytics & Visualisation	37 Infrastructure & Connectivity	38 Cookies, Location & User Data	39 Customer Data & CRM	40 Robotics & Process Automation	41 Artificial Intelligence & Machine Learning	42 Internet of Things & Sensor Data	43 AR, VR & Mixed Reality Interfaces	44 Cloud Apps & Shared Services

Establishing Data Interoperability

digital mindset and changing the way we behave and approach problems, rather than what technology we use, regardless of what roles a person is in. As Mistry's mantra has it, 'you don't have to *do* digital to *be* digital'.

- Are you curious?
- Are you challenging?
- Are you disrupting yourself in the way you think?
- Are you exploring and positively trying to embrace the unknown?

Many principles of the digital mindset are similar and often interchangeable with what psychologist Carol Dweck called a 'growth mindset'.[3] In her words, it 'Is based on the belief that your basic qualities are the things you can cultivate through your efforts. Although people may differ in every which way – their initial talents and aptitudes, interests or temperaments – everyone can change and grow through application and experience.'

All of these are human skills and human traits. If you want to unleash your digital talent, it is crucial to lean into the attributes of the people you already have in the business, framing people's abilities in such a way that it actively encourages innovation.

Digital-first businesses do not have to be technology-led. They have to be people-led. Data will not solve your problems. But people who understand the value of data actually can.

Therefore, the first eleven of these 'human' elements are key to Developing a Digital Mindset: these are ways of thinking which enable employees at all levels to become more open and receptive to change. These are often referred to as 'soft skills', because they are not always considered to be academic or measurable. But in my group discussions with CTOs, there was consensus that 'soft skills' needed a rebrand, as they sound 'fluffy' and less important.

With great strides taken over the last few years in promoting the DE&I agenda in most corporates, and a growing body of research in this area, there is widespread acknowledgement that diversity of thought and approach adds value to business bottom lines and that companies where inclusion flourishes are more profitable.

So I refer to these not as 'soft' but as 'human' skills: unlocking human potential and creating environments where human creativity is able to thrive is good for business.

Developing a Digital Mindset

1. Embracing the Unknown

Fear of change is a perfectly valid, normal human instinct. The prospect of change in any work setting (including changes to processes, expectations, hierarchy or technology) can provoke a natural resistance, which is usually driven by a fear of the unknown: 'Will this new algorithm put my job at risk?', 'Will the new office layout mean I have to sit with people I don't like?', 'Will my new manager share my values or appreciate my work?' Therefore, the first obstacle to changing the way employees operate will be understanding how it affects them, their working day and their career aspirations.

Many working environments, while appearing to function effectively on the surface, are hotbeds of uncertainty and lack the psychological 'safety net' required for people to blindly charge into an unknown future. While in an ideal world, every line manager would have a comprehensive understanding of each member of their team's inner motivations and ultimate career goals, that is rarely the case. Personally, I have worked in companies which talk a good game about being 'just like family', but I have never been as frank around the boardroom table as I have around the dining table, and I've definitely said things to my parents over the years I would never have risked saying to my bosses.

In a workplace setting, the best way to establish this psychological safety is for the leader (whether that is the

CEO, line manager or the leader of the relevant business unit) to credibly give permission for people to fail, without fear of retribution. In some organisations, that permission can be implied, while in others that permission will need to be demonstrated in words (such as policies) and deeds (i.e. publicly celebrating the lessons learned from a project that didn't quite hit its mark), so that members of the team can believe that – while they may be charting an unknown course – they are doing it together. Humans are tribal creatures and seek safety in numbers: everyone feeling they are on the same journey is the fastest way to encourage them to jump on board, whatever the destination.

2. **Openness, Flexibility & Adaptability**
Only once the fear of the unknown is mitigated can the real work begin on approaching change with an open mind, appreciating the diversity of thought already within a team and being willing to try new ways of working.

It can usually be very helpful if leadership drives the openness with integrity and without judgement. You may have been in meetings before where the chair has said 'No idea is a bad idea'... and thought, 'What utter rubbish!' Some ideas are terrible and should definitely be consigned to 'inside voices' status. So if you're a leader and planning to encourage open discussion and questioning of your authority, it is essential that the voices that rise not be silenced (or they may never be heard again).

I was once directly challenged on the viability of one of my ideas by a direct line report, in a meeting, in front of the rest of the team. I didn't particularly enjoy the experience (and she was terrified she had overstepped during her probation period), but I had to concede her point was relevant and we considered her perspective in a group discussion, which enabled us to adapt our roadmap. I was able to reassure her later on that she had never been hired to be a 'yes-person', but because she was the best candidate for her role. Her expertise and opinion was a valid contribution and, though I didn't enjoy her challenge, I appreciated it.

3. **Humility and Emotional Intelligence (EQ)**

Some of the most striking, but least surprising statistics from the research for this book came from the *Corporate AI Capabilities* benchmarking survey. It showed that in the UK's biggest companies, most of which are heavily investing in new artificial intelligence and machine learning technologies, only 9% of senior executives and 3.7% of board members have any experience in technology businesses. This is striking because it seems low but not particularly surprising because for most of those firms, technology is an enabler, rather than a core part of their business offering.

One statistic that was fairly shocking, however, came from the first survey I ran, where I discovered that fewer than one in four CEOs, boards and senior executives, 'Fully understand and trust the data they use to make strategic decisions with'. It is impossible to solve a problem if you don't understand what it is and this widespread problem in Britain's boardrooms demonstrates that it isn't just you and your team who 'don't know what they don't know': it's your bosses and their bosses, and their bosses too...

This is where humility comes in. If you have eliminated fear of the unknown and developed openness, flexibility and adaptability, it is time to appreciate that, however well you and your team understand your roles, and however persuasively you may be able describe the precise value your work brings to the business overall, you may not be able to for long. With uncertainty, change and new ways of working will undoubtedly come new things to learn, new approaches to adopt and these may have significant impacts on what your day-to-day activities look like. Admitting that we don't know what we don't know and being emotionally open to new stimuli can bring very positive change, if we allow it.

For example, if your company installs a new system which means that data entry becomes more seamless and automated, which now takes you five hours less per week... do you see this is as a threat or an opportunity? According to Parkinson's Law,[4] work will always expand to fill the time available. Will you use this change to do five hours' less work a week, or find an exciting new project to fill five hours a week? Or will you focus on expanding more interesting parts of your role, spending more time being creative, and therefore making your work better and more fulfilling? Approaching this question with humility (rather than defensiveness) could bring far greater job satisfaction and impact.

4. Entrepreneurship

Some organisations are, by design, more entrepreneurial than others. Entrepreneurs are broadly defined as those who start a business or who are far-sighted risk-takers. Personally I take my meaning from its French origin, 'entreprendre', which literally means to 'undertake', or to 'get shit done'. However you take your definition, entrepreneurship is about putting thought into action and actually achieving what others may only be brave enough to think about. Entrepreneurship is about having the courage of your convictions, putting your money where your mouth is and believing you can be the person to make stuff happen.

I see entrepreneurship as the flipside element to humility. If you can be brave enough to recognise what you don't know, that you need to embark on a learning journey, I believe that being an entrepreneur in this context means you can also be brave enough to recognise that there is good stuff you do already know and – combined with new approaches and new learning – you have what it takes to be successful in your new 'undertaking'.

5. Design Thinking

The Interaction Design Foundation describes Design Thinking as, 'A non-linear, iterative process that teams use to understand users, challenge assumptions, redefine problems and create innovative solutions to prototype and test. It is most useful to tackle ill-defined or unknown problems and involves five phases: Empathise, Define, Ideate, Prototype and Test.'[5]

Being able to look at problems from new angles (whether on your own or as part of a team) is essential to developing a digital mindset.

6. Diversity, Equity & Inclusion

There are many types of diversity in every workplace and recognising that everyone in your team brings with them differing viewpoints, backgrounds, beliefs, goals and life experiences is incredibly helpful in deconstructing 'groupthink' (the mode of thinking that people engage in when they are deeply involved in a cohesive 'in-group'), and identifying solutions that can be beneficial for more than a single, homogenous 'end-user'.

To promote equity in a working environment is about far more than ensuring people are paid the right amount: it enables each of those diverse voices to be able to contribute in the best way that they can, ensuring the whole team has equal access to new ways of working and communicating. It also lays the foundation stone for people being able to 'speak truth to power' (covered in the behaviour elements), by beginning to flatten hierarchical power dynamics that could discourage innovation.

While diversity and equity may be about uncovering the many and varied human contributions your organisation has access to, inclusion is about creating the space for those thoughts and ideas to flourish, without fear of being squashed, silenced or manipulated. A truly inclusive working environment is one where employees can bring their 'whole selves to work' and is critical in beginning to unlock the value that variety can provide.

7. Agile and Lean Methodology

All 21st century organisations have had to evolve to thrive in an unpredictable, rapidly changing, intrinsically networked environment. Agile ones embrace change by focusing on customers: embedding customer-centricity in all they do. They create light-touch processes and practices that can fluidly adapt and adjust to changes in the market, technology, regulation and feedback. They are inclusive and open with flattened hierarchies, evolving continuously, without the disruption caused by restructuring to adapt, as is often the case in more traditional organisations. This approach enables employees to embrace uncertainty and ambiguity with greater confidence.

Working hand-in-glove with Agile environments is the Lean methodology, which facilitates an ongoing process of incremental adjustment, significantly accelerating product delivery by making the most of resources and effort, enabling teams to work more effectively and efficiently.

One of the five key recommendations from PA Consulting's survey of 500 leaders from large global organisations was to embrace Agility across the workforce, but the report noted that is easier said than done:[6] '60% of leaders said they knew their organisations needed to change, but that embedding and scaling up agility was a struggle. Agility confronts teams and leaders with totally new ways of working. It demands the ripping up of much of what is taken for granted today. It entails the merging of functions, teams or areas, the creation of new departments and redesigned processes – whether it's managing performance and suppliers or drawing up budgets.'

Agile adds value. Research from McKinsey & Company showed that businesses which successfully harness Agile are 1.5 times more likely to report financial outperformance relative to peers and 1.7 times more likely to outperform in non-financial terms.[7]

However, even if you work in an organisation which is resistant to a total culture change, or where there are structural barriers which prevent its adoption, merely adopting the most basic principles of Agile and Lean can add value. But what it will undoubtedly bring is tremendous focus: on end results, on better products and services, and on achieving more with less. This is how you can begin to think like a startup.

8. Thinking Like a Startup

As with Agile and Lean, many thousands of words have been written about how to think like a startup. But from my personal experience, having worked in both startups and major corporates, the key differentiators are that in startup culture: (a) decision making takes way less time, (b) obstacles are easier to overcome, and (c) the appetite for risk is infinitely higher.

The first two of these are simply virtues of size. Economies of scale mean that larger organisations have grown to doing certain things in certain ways because eliminating variety (in system design, customer experience, product quality) is the best way to guarantee consistency, with a minimum of human oversight. Thinking like a startup within the context of an enterprise-scale firm is usually far more about working out (with the right stakeholders) which rules can be broken and which can be bent, so your team can innovate without anyone getting fired. As for risk appetite, I will cover that in element 10.

9. Experimentation

Children are able to imagine with fewer boundaries than adults, precisely because they are able to experiment without fear of failure or rejection. Bringing in an element of play and experimentation is an integral part of enabling a data mindset, because it helps to develop a sense of psychological safety. One of the leaders in this field is LEGO®, which a few years ago developed SERIOUS PLAY®: an experiential process designed for use in guided workshops with adults to prompt dialogue and encourage reflection, as well as develop problem-solving skills and use of the imagination.

10. Risk Awareness

One of the single biggest barriers to innovation in any established corporate entity – though this is particularly true for organisations which operate in highly regulated environments, like financial services – is risk aversion. This is what makes risk appetite one of the key differentiators between startups and established corporations. Senior executives (especially those whose decisions can impact shareholder value) are conditioned to weigh every change in process against the prospect of harm it could inadvertently deliver.

In these environments, before one can test – and stretch – the boundaries of a company's risk appetite, one first needs to understand the challenges those senior decision-makers are facing. Some risks are very real, many are imagined, but all have a valid place in the minds of those who are responsible for their implications.

Which is why Risk Awareness is an important, but often overlooked, element of developing a digital mindset. While most data innovators within companies will have come across risk-aversion in colleagues, risk awareness is about flipping that instinct upside down, asking, 'Why... really, why?' and working to understand the root cause of the feared implications that each risk poses. In some cases, it may be simply our first building block: a need to embrace the unknown, but in many cases, asking, 'Why... really, why?' can help you identify individual sub-risks or dangerous obstacles which can be overcome or mitigated with a collaborative approach.

Bridging this gap is critical in ensuring executive buy-in, sponsorship and support for any new strategy or data-related innovation.

11. Data Literacy

While the first ten elements are all foundational knowledge building blocks to developing a digital mindset, data literacy is the 'bridge' to embedding new behaviours. Data literacy can sound to non-geeks (like your author) like a terrifying new skill-set to be mastered, but it doesn't require you to drop everything and attend a six-week coding bootcamp! Data literacy is all about understanding *How*, *Where*, *When* and *Why* your organisation uses data. Only once you have an appreciation of your business's current data state and limitations, can you start to envisage a way forward and begin to imagine the art of the possible.

Not everyone can or will be able to adopt all of these elements, all of the time. But in understanding the Periodic Table as a starting point, it is nearly always possible to ensure that across a team or function, all bases can be covered, meaning that teamwork and group dynamics will benefit from the diversity of approaches.

The most important step-change is for organisation leaders to recognise the need to create a positive environment where these ways of thinking can be possible, without fear of judgement or retaliation.

By observing and becoming aware of the first eleven elements of the Periodic Table, businesses can begin creating a place of psychological safety, where openness, entrepreneurship and experimentation can be encouraged, rather than feared. Using these knowledge building blocks, businesses of all shapes and sizes can start on their journey to celebrating innovation, by beginning to embed data innovation behaviours.

Embedding Data Innovation Behaviours

12. Lifelong Learning

When teams and individuals have a digital mindset, the behaviour of continuous learning should follow quite naturally. In their 2011 book *Put Your Mindset to Work*, authors James Reed and Paul Stoltz explored research with thousands of employers into the perceived differences between skills and mindset. The overall message of the book is that mindset is of far higher importance to recruiters and managers globally, as role-specific skills can be taught far more easily, especially to those who have curious, inquiring mindsets.

One of their key messages is around accountability, which reflects Agile methodology: 'What do employers mean when they say they want people to be accountable? At work we are all accountable to someone. Every organisation is accountable to its customers. Individual members of staff are accountable to one another. The chief executive is accountable to the board and the board is accountable to the owners. In great companies, *everyone* is accountable to the customer.'

While the provision of adequate training is a requirement for any organisation wanting their employees to continue to develop and grow, remember this is the first of our behavioural elements, so Lifelong Learning is about meeting individual ambition, not the employer's mandatory expectations. This behaviour is about seeking knowledge, about wanting to understand new opportunities, angles or advancements in technology and how they can be brought into the process of innovation. Embedding continuous learning is how you can ensure your team are accountable to each other and everyone is accountable to the customer.

13. Fostering Collaboration

When seeking knowledge, where better than to seek it than from your peers? Learning can be a lonely experience, but decades of extensive research has consistently shown that being able to demonstrate and share knowledge with each other is far more effective at embedding new learning in practical, useable ways. By encouraging your teams to work together on projects and discuss their learnings, they will all be able to enhance them with additional insights and may find new ways to apply novel concepts in your organisation's working environment.

14. Building Networks and Communities

The old idiom 'When the tide rises, all boats rise' is never truer than when applied to group education. Establishing informal, grassroots communities of people with similar interests, or by building more targeted peer-to-peer learning networks of people with similar responsibilities (especially across different functions), can have a profound impact on new knowledge adoption and massively accelerate data innovation by bringing together complementary perspectives and enthusiasm.

15. Exploring Possibility Together

Whether you and your teams create formal or informal groups to support each other's development, or whether you just work together on innovation projects that put the digital mindset into practice (both of which are perfectly valid approaches – everybody has their own learning style), the most important concept is to explore possibility together.

This leads on from the mindset elements of humility, openness and DE&I: once you have enabled the voices to speak up and listen to each other, take joy in the opportunity to meet new opportunities with wide-eyed enthusiasm. Put your experimentation element to good use and give yourselves permission to PLAY with ideas!

16. Sharing Ideas and Good Practices

It isn't just play you can share: after all, you're not actually children! You are professionals, with years (perhaps decades) of collective institutional memory, relevant business insight and knowledge of established ways of working you can disrupt together.

Once you're in a safe space to innovate and you're collaborating effectively, don't miss the opportunity to share ideas about the practical stuff: business objectives which could be enhanced, profits which could be improved, supply chains that could be optimised, common corporate barriers which could be overcome, ancient processes which could be radically overhauled.

17. Engaging and Empowering

'No one can make you feel inferior without your consent.'
Eleanor Roosevelt

It is easy to presume that empowerment must come from the top – and it is true that innovation cannot exist in a controlled vacuum – there is definitely a role for CEOs, board members and leaders to play in 'permissioning' innovative behaviours. But many years ago, my first leadership coach told me something so profoundly obvious, I have never been able to disprove it: 'Power must be taken, it cannot be given.' If you want to take control of your destiny, you cannot wait for someone else to give you permission to do so.

Back in 2006, academics Fook, White & Gardner pointed out the risks of engaging many voices in a team, if you're not prepared to pay attention to them:[8] 'Employees, at times, also rightly feel that the experience of being "empowered" by reflection, and therefore being more visible or vocal in the organisation, can have unwanted and sometimes painful consequences.'

In order to be a data innovation leader, you must embody the mindset elements of DE&I and humility, by creating a safe space for your team to challenge – you, your assumptions, the status quo – in order to be able to imagine what 'better' looks like. By using a flat-hierarchy approach to the team dynamic, where every voice has a place and it is possible to put forward views without fear of judgement or retribution, each member of the team (at whatever level in the organisation) can actively work to engage, elevate and empower each other.

18. Using Data to Drive Decision-Making

Before you can pitch in an innovative solution to most problem-owners, you may need to demonstrate the problem in cold, hard numbers. Even if you don't, being able to illustrate a problem space with facts is excellent practice.

One of the potential down-sides of all this play, experimentation and new product ideation can be an over-reliance on 'gut instinct', which is the most common human reaction to identifying a problem space: we can often 'feel' an issue before we can accurately describe it. And 'gut instinct' is often the biggest 'red flag' for a decision-maker who is conditioned by the organisation's risk appetite. It is also the hardest to defend. Remember: it isn't personal. The person or people who can stop you taking unnecessary risks are doing their jobs by spotting the Achilles heel in your plan!

So if you and your team believe a problem to exist, and you want to be given permission to solve it using data innovation, you have a responsibility to be able to illustrate the problem using objective empirical data points, rather than relying on subjective, anecdotal or circumstantial evidence.

19. Being Braver and Bolder

A team which is engaged and empowered will find greater influence in a collective voice: by respecting different approaches and opinions, a diverse group which can land on a popular solution will stand a far greater chance of being able to argue it from concept to reality.

One of the most effective exercises I use in workshops is for the group to imagine a shared 'future state' where the problem is solved. The imagination is a powerful tool and being able to envisage the solution makes understanding the steps to reaching it less fanciful and more pragmatic. This simple shift can make even the boldest, bravest steps seem practical and intuitive.

By encouraging everyone to collaborate effectively, be aware of risk, establish good practice and have the courage of their convictions, a team can move from thinking like entrepreneurs, to acting like them. Early successes, using data to drive decision-making and a sense of strength in numbers will enable them to become gradually bolder and braver in their ideas and, ultimately, able to speak truth to power.

Speaking truth to power is a crucial development in being able to move from innovation as a concept to innovation in practice. The collaborative development of knowledge and group ideation should lead to a sense of belief in, and collective responsibility for, the solutions proposed. Being able to honestly challenge the status quo and offer the purse-holders and risk-owners constructive, novel solutions can create a paradigm shift for all involved.

20. Becoming Pioneers Together

When it comes to strength in numbers, it isn't just your team who need to rally together. For any data innovation to make it from concept to practical delivery, you will need to bring in other people: executive sponsors, end-users and champions across your organisation.

This is where collaborators become co-conspirators. It is important to bring others along on the journey with you so that innovation doesn't become a weapon which may be perceived to be in the wrong hands. Align your data innovation with existing corporate strategy and demonstrate how your solutions can add value (and possibly glory) to people outside of your immediate team. There is always a danger that data innovation will be seen as 'Us vs. Them', so be mindful of this perception and ensure that the 'Them' in question is the actual problem, not just the people who own the problem. By fighting the old ways together, you can bathe other stakeholders in the halo effect of this pioneering spirit.

21. Being Responsive to New Information

When developing the elements of a digital mindset, you learned to embrace the unknown, you approached new ideas with humility and you respected alternative viewpoints. When it comes to pitching in your novel solution, it pays to be mindful of the human tendency – we all have at times – to regress to being a know-it-all.

So, you have collaborated, sought input, gathered data to support your assumptions, become aware of risks and thought like a startup. By this point you probably have a strong sense of belief in your solution and are becoming confident in speaking truth to power. So when your senior decision-maker says 'No' at this point and refuses to let you proceed any further, it is easy to take the rejection personally, to dig in and make your points more emphatically, to think your stakeholder is short-sighted or blinded by profits... or just plain stupid.

Stop. Perhaps there is information you do not have access to, or forces outside of anyone's control mean your solution just isn't viable. It may feel you have only two options at this point: (a) argue until you get fired, or (b) give up entirely. But there is always a third way. Remember what you have learned so far. Explore (c): rather than throwing the baby out with the bathwater, find out more. Investigate the circumstances. Approach your stakeholder with humility and understand his or her objections. Be receptive and responsive to new information. Then go back to the drawing board and see whether you can use that new information to make your solution even more kickass.

22. Embracing Positive Disruption

Remember the first mindset element: embracing the unknown? Fear of change is a perfectly valid, normal human instinct. By this point, you will have established the difference between disruption for positive change and disruption for its own sake. As you begin to design and build solutions to organisational problems, creating disruption is inevitable. Being mindful of this, you should work to ensure that change is experienced by others in the context of building more positive outcomes.

As academics Helen Storey and Mathilde Joubert explained when discussing collaboration:[9] 'You have to be prepared to open up and truly take that other person into account, and not become prescriptive to them. And that's where the risk is, because they can come up with something that you don't like. The ideal scenario is that you come up with the third idea that neither of you have thought of on your own.'

Being able to embrace positive disruption is an important element in your communications toolkit: being able to demonstrate your awareness of risk, your flexibility and your data-driven decision-making, your role here is to empathise with others who may be adversely affected, to help them to understand the net-positive impact of the change on how they perform their roles. It is also worth bearing in mind how disrupting their roles may also have a net-positive impact on the organisation's overall objectives: if they can see the impact of the value they add (and a place for themselves in the new world order), they may be far more amenable to embracing the change themselves.

23. Taking Risks

In earlier elements, we explored the importance of being aware of risk, how to use data to make more informed decisions, while sharing ideas and good practices. Having brought other people along on the journey and encouraged people to get on board with positive disruption, now is the time to use what you have learned by applying boldness and bravery, by taking measured, reasonable risks.

If all has gone well, by now, you will have surrounded yourself with people who are prepared to jump off the cliff with you. But in order to lead, you need to believe enough in what you're trying to do, to be ready to jump first.

24. Failing Fast

Data innovation will not be successful 100% of the time. The level of failure acceptable in different working environments will vary hugely: some extremely data-mature companies I have interviewed have pitched their expected failure rate at 20–30%, while others are closer to 50% (or one in every two innovations).

Largely this will depend on the amount of rigour and process that surrounds the practice of data innovation, but often it will simply be a case of the amount a company is willing to invest in experimentation before pulling the plug. The CTO in a major telecommunications firm I interviewed said she looks for a 60% success rate on novel data projects as standard.

Whatever your organisation's appetite for failure (or whether you are establishing its very first fail-friendly process), the aim should be to mirror the startup playbook by failing fast, so that you mitigate the level of investment required to reach very clearly defined success or failure milestones.

You can support this by having very transparent processes, so that your team approaches data innovation through the lens of exploring possibility, rather than depending on a viable solution. It is important that you all buy-in to failure as a viable option so you feel free enough to take those big leaps off the cliffs without worrying about the rocks below.

Of course, for many major corporates, acceptance of failure at all will seem counter-cultural, with executives only willing to sign off on experiments if there is some guarantee of success. In these situations, it may help to adopt a 'gated' approach. This is where product development is designed to have five 'gates', with clearly marked milestones, which allow a project to pass on to the next stage. This limits the company's exposure to failure by only committing enough resources for each phase. Implementing this process will also help to convince dissenters that failure can be managed within acceptable boundaries.

The following illustration shows an adaptation of the gated delivery process, developed by British-American technologist Ian Whitford, for use in deploying novel technologies at-scale in industrial environments. I have witnessed this gated approach first-hand, being used successfully in company-wide development and deployment of machine learning products.

Gate X: Experiment
- Understand the opportunity and determine feasibility.
- Work with stakeholders to understand the business impact.
- Undertake a horizon scan of alternative solutions.

Gate 0: Define MVP
- Understand requirements needed for Minimum Viable Product (including data).
- Establish & agree potential value and associated risks.
- Identify primary stakeholder and put together project team

Gate 1: Build & Validate MVP
- Build MVP and confirm business case (re-baselining value statement if necessary).
- Release MVP to a limited user group for testing & validation.
- Determine that primary stakeholder is satisfied with process for value calculation.

Gate 2: Refine Product
- Working in sprints, release new features in accordance with product backlog.
- Expand the number of users.
- Track the value realised by the product.
- Determine if the solution can be applied in other business areas.

Gate 3: Productionise
- Establish productionisation team.
- Define and commit to a productionisation plan.
- Start to hand over related knowledge artefacts and train users to run the product without assistance.

25. Learning Through Feedback Loops

To stretch the cliff metaphor even further, the most important thing to learn from failure is how to keep improving the way you jump. Mistakes can be expensive – in time, money and credibility – so it is vitally important you learn not to repeat your mistakes. We do this by fully documenting the data innovation process so that we learn to recognise the patterns by using feedback loops, constantly reviewing the process so we can see what went wrong, where, when and why. That way, the next time we launch into an experiment, we can avoid earlier pitfalls and improve our chance of success next time around.

26. Iterating Better Solutions

To approach any data innovation is to be prepared to try, try and try again, until you get it right. Failure isn't an end; it is often a necessary milestone towards success. Every time you fail, you learn a lesson and try something slightly better the next time.

The first 26 elements in the Periodic Table are designed to be flexible and not overly prescriptive, so they can be viewed as a simple, scalable framework which caters for all learners, skill levels and domain expertise. Implementing this framework across a team is the fastest way to develop a clear understanding of the mindset and behaviours a group of colleagues need to get started on their journey, providing everyone with a 'safe space to do hard things', regardless of their background or prior experience.

By applying this framework, individuals can begin to understand how their personal drivers, their purpose and their desire for growth can add to the overall data strategy, outlined in the next section.

Understanding Data as a Strategic Asset

When a group's digital mindset and data innovation behaviours have been developed, the organisation can really start to identify the strengths and weaknesses in its data value chain.

27. Data Quality and Hygiene

'Rubbish in, rubbish out' is the commonly used warning when it comes to making decisions with data. Put simply, the quality of the decisions you can make, the products you can design and the solutions you can build will be informed by the quality of the data you have at your disposal.

Data quality and hygiene is a problem in businesses of all sizes (and ages), but is particularly prevalent in organisations which are large, old and complex. Over the course of decades, many businesses have grown by virtue of mergers and acquisitions, creating a complicated web of often interdependent legacy systems with different requirements, inputs, formats, ages, languages and quality. Left unmanaged (and in many cases these systems can be so overwhelmingly large that they appear entirely unmanageable), the resulting data can easily become out-of-date, unreliable and difficult to access.

Data hygiene can also be subject to external forces. In 2018, organisations across Europe (and global companies trying to market to European customers) faced into what many called the 'GDPR Apocalypse', when a change in data protection laws caused firms to ask their customers to opt back in to receiving marketing information from them, or expect hefty fines of up to €20m (about £18m) or 4% of annual global turnover, whichever was the greater.

The result was an enforced cleansing of customer relationship management data worldwide, which has mostly been seen as a blessing in disguise. The GDPR regulations also required businesses to state within their policies how long a customer's data could 'reasonably' be kept, requiring them to 'expire' data which was no longer current and remove it from their systems.

Of course, for many organisations, customer data is merely the tip of the iceberg and there have been no similarly sweeping regulatory requirements for other types of data (among them product design, manufacturing schematics, financial information) to be kept neat and tidy. The challenge this creates for data strategists is that in most corporate environments, it is incredibly difficult to understand what value may be hiding in plain sight, within the data sets that already exist across a firm's enterprise estate. Cleaning and making accessible the data sets you use to make decisions with is the first (often painful) step to more adequately establishing your data integrity.

28. Data Integrity

When your data is clean, you can start to have faith in the decisions you use it to make and encourage confidence in your predictions. Data integrity refers to the maintenance and the assurance of data, ensuring it is accurate and consistent across its life cycle. Systems which process, store or retrieve data are dependent on data integrity in order for you to design, implement or use it moving forwards.

While quality and hygiene of existing data sets concern themselves with the current state of play, data integrity is far more about understanding the strengths and weaknesses in inputs, outputs and the ways data is used across your organisation, to ensure that future data strategy is developed without the need for further retrospective cleansing.

29. Data Ethics

Gary Marcus, author of *Taming Silicon Valley*, said 'The people who are running AI don't really care that much about what you might call responsible AI, and that the consequences for society may be severe.'

While data integrity focuses on ensuring your data is gathered, interrogated and stored in ways that your business can trust, the ethical use of data tends to involve broader moral concerns about how to protect your business and its stakeholders (customers, users, patients, staff etc.) from potential harms which may arise from the ways you collect, store and apply that data.

Long recognised as a field of academic study (I first started working with professors of digital ethics in around 2015), in recent years – in part due to 2018's GDPR legislation – data ethics has finally become a board-level concern, especially in public-facing organisations that recognise the level of their dependency on data. That isn't to say that there is a widespread understanding of what data ethics is, or what good data ethics actually looks like, but since 2017 it has made regular appearances on corporate risk registers as something that needs to be mitigated by general good practice.

The problem here is that most companies don't fully understand the many and varied ways they collect and use data. A number of our mindset and behavioural elements can help with developing a clearer understanding of data ethics in your working environment, from embracing the unknown and data literacy, to lifelong learning and building networks and communities. The element that plays the biggest role in developing your data ethics, however, is probably diversity, equity and inclusion. Interestingly, in several of the businesses I work with, data ethics is seen as the part of the Chief Operating Officer's remit (as part of the DE&I or CSR strategy), rather than as part of the Chief Technology Officer's.

Wherever it sits in your organisation, it is crucial to have a clear line of sight of what is and isn't ethical when developing your data strategy. Understanding how good data ethics can support overall business strategy, help mitigate corporate risks and drive more ethical data innovation will be profoundly helpful in building a data strategy which considers the 'purpose' or corporate social responsibility elements of your board's long-term vision.

30. Cyber Security & Resilience

Most companies with a staff development or continuous learning programmes will have basic modules on things like Cyber Essentials, and many large businesses (certainly all those with ISO27001 credentials) will have programmes in place to support cyber resilience, such as regular network penetration testing. However, regardless of size, having policies and practices in place to protect the resilience of your systems and the integrity of your data, as well as the security of data associated with your people, your customers and your products, is essential to shoring up its value. This level of assurance will help with starting to quantify your data as a strategic business asset.

31. Data Engineering & Architecture

This is the first of three elements which require either technical computational abilities or an understanding of how to manage the people in your business who have them. Data architecture describes the blueprint by which data is managed, from collection and storage through to transformation, sharing and use. It sets the ways data flows through the organisation. Engineering is the practice of managing that flow, whether the data is stored in unrelated silos or in data 'warehouses' or 'lakes'. Any comprehensive data strategy needs to account for how and where it is stored, and who is accountable for its storage and movement.

32. Programming and Software Inputs

The second technical oversight element, software and hardware programming is the process of designing and building executable computer programmes, which accomplish specific results. In order for these to complement and enhance the overall organisational objectives, the data strategy needs to include a clear plan for how new data inputs will be designed and executed.

33. Data Science & Innovation

The third technical element involves the further interrogation of, and innovation with, data across your platforms, systems and programmes, blending those technical capabilities with the earlier elements of positive disruption, failing fast, learning and iterating. Data science is how we develop a deeper understanding of the potential hiding within data sets and can, through experimentation, begin to develop products and solutions which push the boundaries of the possible.

34. Data Governance

Embedding comprehensive data governance processes and protocols is key to establishing the accountability of a corporate data strategy. Bringing together the last few elements, good data governance will clearly outline the accessibility, integrity and security of a business's data, usually through a set of agreed policies and standards. In short, data governance sets the rules about how a business's data collection and storage will interact with the outside world.

35. Internal & External User Experience

Having established the baseline of how your organisation intends for its data to interact with others, you will need to consider how those end users will engage with your platforms, channels and systems in return. While terms like 'customer experience' (CX), 'user experience' (UX) or 'user interface' (UI) may sound like jargon only relevant for

Silicon Valley startups looking to launch a new app, every computational system or platform depends on users at some point in its gathering, processing or using of data.

Many of the CTOs and CIOs I have spoken to, from some of the world's biggest companies, had tragic stories of well-imagined, brilliant and necessary data innovations that had withered on the vine because the product design stage hadn't done enough to consider the actual needs and behaviours of the people who would be ultimately using them.

36. Management Information, Analytics and Data Visualisation

Also critical to consider, if you want your data innovations to be successful, are not just the end users of your product, but the senior stakeholders who may be looking for very specific results from a successful deployment.

There is a growing dependence on data in the boardroom: my research showed that 87% of senior executives and board members feel that Management Information (MI) has become more complex over the last few years, with 70% saying they have become more reliant on data analytics and AI for their MI over the same period. Meanwhile, 78% of leaders say they expect to be 'largely' or 'completely' reliant on data to make business decisions moving forwards.

As helpful as it would be for board members and the C-suite to also learn and adopt the mindset and behaviour elements detailed here, very few organisations are in a position to make that a reality. Therefore, in order for you to effectively communicate what you need senior managers, executives and stakeholders to *interpret* from the data you provide them with, you first need to appreciate what they *believe* they need from data. Sometimes, you just need to deliver your messages in language, charts or images that they will recognise and understand.

This is why so much of my coaching work with corporate technologists centres on bridging the communication gaps between 'those who speak data' and 'those who speak business'. The way you present MI, analytics and data visualisation will often determine whether a project gets a green light, regardless of the value it may represent.

The reason this is the final element in the Understanding Data as a Strategic Asset section, is because this management information and data presentation is how you communicate that value to the stakeholders who probably don't share your level of insight, your mindset or your behaviours, so it is your job to help them understand the value of the data in your organisation.

Establishing Data Interoperability

Developing a digital mindset encourages people within an organisation to think differently; embedding data innovation behaviours offers them the opportunity to apply new approaches to problems; understanding data as a strategic asset enables an organisation to understand the value it has, often hiding in plain sight. All of these elements make it possible to apply data innovation in a targeted way: they may well be enough for a small company, or a division of a business to innovate in a silo.

However, because a significant amount of my work has been with major global corporates, the Data Strategy Alliance working groups have identified a particular set of elements which apply to enterprise-scale deployment of data innovation. Therefore, the final eight elements focus on considering how data is collected and used across an enterprise estate. These are particularly relevant for larger, older, multinational corporations, but I recognise some or most of them may only be of passing interest to businesses which have not reached the same scale. So below are included broad overviews of the principal channels through which data finds its way into most organisations... and where it often gets stuck through lack of interoperability.

The big challenge here for organisations large enough to have to consider some, most or all of the below elements, will be working out where to focus when building a comprehensive data strategy. Enabling data innovation in one department, product area or silo is difficult enough, without needing to consider the interoperability between different – sometimes competing or conflicting – systems. Geography can also provide a barrier for large corporates: some of these channels may be based in separate countries, impacted by different legislation, or run and processed in a variety of languages.

37. Infrastructure and Connectivity

Every organisation has both physical and virtual infrastructure that generate data and impact the overall data strategy. Physical infrastructure can involve heavily mechanised factories, high-specification scientific technology, multi-user point of sale devices, warehoused data centres, or simply offices full of computer equipment. How these things are connected to each other, how they generate, store and transmit data and the rate at which these physical or hardware items are expected to depreciate (and need replacing or upgrading) will all be essential to a comprehensive data strategy.

38. Robotics and Process Automation

This element focuses on the types of automation prevalent in primary industries (such as manufacturing, engineering, precision tooling), rather than customer- or service-focused automation, which is covered in later elements.

The types of business where process automation and developments in robotics are high priorities, tend to be older and larger, with well-established dependencies on manual processes and where there are major strategic or financial benefits to be made from efficiency gains and optimisation at-scale.

Existing robotisation and automation may have been bought in or could be the result of successful previous data innovations. Whether your data strategy encompasses new automation projects, or just the ongoing maintenance of existing ones, it will need to factor in the way data flows through the systems, what it tells you and how you use that information for better product design for future use.

39. Cookies, Location and User Data

Understanding how your company collects, stores, processes and utilises data generated by customers or end-users (either through software, hardware, apps or websites) is important from a data governance point of view, but we concern ourselves here with how those customer-facing systems interact with your other data channels, and whether the data taken from these sources is interoperable. Does your organisation track how end-users 'play' with your products and services? And is that data used for ongoing product design and development, or merely for tailoring marketing messages from the communications team?

40. Customer Data and CRM Systems

Most organisations use some sort of customer relationship management (CRM) system, whether it is a cloud-based app or a proprietorial system developed specifically for your customer environment. These systems are the ones most likely to be regularly cleansed (due to regulatory requirements), but is the data being adequately used to improve customer experiences, or for process enhancements? Is your customer data deliberately ringfenced in a separate silo to keep it secure? What value could be unlocked if this data was blended (even if in aggregate, anonymised ways) with your AI tools, or other customer touchpoints?

41. Artificial Intelligence and Machine Learning

My research has shown that a third of business leaders feel they are investing more heavily in AI, machine learning and data science than their closest market competitors, while 75% expect their firms to increase investment in over the next few years. The potential for artificial intelligence to transform organisations – particularly large corporations with significant data sets – is huge. And that potential grows exponentially when these technologies are applied across silos, rather than keeping them focused on a limited number of purposes.

42. Internet of Things and Sensor Data

At senior levels in many established businesses, talk of IoT has diminished over the last couple years as newer, cooler technologies (blockchain and generative AI to name just two) have grabbed the headlines. However, a huge number of large engineering, electrical and manufacturing firms have been embedding sensors into the physical products they make and sell for years now, and the data is piling up.

The CTO at a well-known automotive firm told me they generate so much data, globally, from the sensors in their vehicles, that they would need to invest heavily in supercompute capability, just to be able to process or understand the volumes. He said, 'While we're certain there is a huge amount of value hiding in the data, we don't know what it is, or whether it'll help us sell more cars, so the investment is a tough sell.'

43. Augmented, Virtual and Mixed Reality Interfaces

Augmented Reality (AR), Virtual reality (VR) and Mixed Reality (XR) platforms are not exclusive to cool startups and Big Tech firms: the technologies are becoming more readily integrated into many traditional forms of manufacture, design and medicine. Increasingly, the use of these is driving the digitisation of some of the oldest and least accessible types of data that many firms have: hand drawn schematics and designs. The use of AR, VR and XR (along with other innovations like 3D printing) have enabled the way some companies produce and make things to leapfrog from the 19th to the 21st century in a single jump.

The kinds of data these platforms both rely on and create could be hugely valuable for those firms and the potential for data innovation is enormous if they can be blended with other data sets.

44. Cloud Applications and Shared Services

Most modern enterprise businesses depend on outsourcing some of the technology-driven services they use to firms which specialise in software to handle specific problems (such as accounting, CRM, voice/call-centre automation). From the companies I have interviewed, it varies whether the deployment of such systems sits within the budgets of a central technology function, or in siloed business divisions. And in many cases, their use is so widespread and integral to the jobs being performed that they are often not seen as technology at all.

But they are data channels, being used to process, store and often present data which can inform business decisions in ways that are unrelated (and possibly running contrary) to your company's overall data strategy. A comprehensive strategy will find a way to integrate these feeds and insights, blending them with data from other sources and channels.

9

The Data Success Framework

Working through the Periodic Table will give you a pretty clear idea about where your organisation is on its journey to data transformation. Understanding its data maturity can also help you identify the right people across the business to help take you from where you are to the next stage. As PA Consulting said in its Agile report, 'From the outset, it's crucial to identify the expertise needed and potential gaps. Requisitioning and ringfencing the appropriate in-house skills is a start, but looking outside can help inspire and support this talent on their journey, especially in the early stages.'

Engaging your communicators

When I run in-house workshops and training sessions with clients, I actively encourage them to bring in their PR, government affairs or marketing people. The importance of engaging communications professionals as part of your 'transformation squad' is two-fold. Firstly, they generally have a holistic view of the whole company, focused as they are on communicating the strengths of organisation-wide strategy to the outside world, while concealing its weaknesses; and secondly, they are often extroverts (or 'people people') and are likely to already be influential, with strong networks and multi-level stakeholder relationships across the firm.

You don't have to *be* digital to *do* digital and there are a host of ways communications professionals can support your organisation's transformation journey, first among which is recognising the many different ways the humans in your business understand, respond to and advocate for change. Leveraging those relationships and networks and taking expert advice on how to communicate change – internally as well as externally – is always helpful.

Almost every workforce has a blend of 'old-timers' and 'newbies': you are just as likely to come across fevered enthusiasts going through their first transformation programme as you are to find hardened veterans with what is referred to as 'transformation fatigue', depending on where they have worked before, and how many times they feel they've been through the ringer.

These in-house workshops are always telling. If you get the blend of personalities right, you can identify fairly quickly where the challenges to an organisation's change programme are. As an ice-breaker, I often ask teams to write on a piece of paper how successful they feel the company's change communications are, on a scale of 1 to 10. Inevitably, the closer a person works to the CEO or executive team, they are more likely to believe they are 'smashing it' with an 8 or 9, while workers closer to the action are likely be struggling on a 2 or 3.

You can't expect all of the people to be in the same place: transformation can be hugely unsettling and I've yet to come across any organisation that has such a strong sense of psychological safety that it can't be shaken by rearranging someone's working day.

I had dinner recently with a friend who runs change communications in a big insurance company, who told me what a total shambles their transformation was. However, when I interviewed his CIO for my research, he happily told me the change programme was a huge success and that he had total buy-in and consensus, so it varies according to your perspective.

In this chapter, we will explore the Data Success Framework, developed with CTOs and CIOs in some of the world's most successful businesses, which outlines the ten metrics the research shows are the best indicators of a brilliant transformation programme.

And five of those metrics depend on excellent communications with employees and stakeholders, from 'inspiring change' and 'including people' to 'embedding data strategy' and 'promoting lifelong learning'.

Tapping into the earlier elements from the Periodic Table, what you are looking for in potential collaborators across your organisation are the personality traits often found in communications professionals: resilience, ability to persuade, negotiating skills and being able to read a room.

A propensity towards our first element, embracing uncertainty, will also be hugely beneficial. Being collaborative is obviously important. If you're asking your colleagues to keep an open mind to the benefits of transformation, it helps if you can expose yourself slightly, to show that you're open to input and ideas. While you shouldn't lose sight of your goals, you should be prepared to be a little flexible as to how you reach them. It's okay to have a target destination in mind, but to be satisfied if you only get people halfway there. Bank the results where you can find them.

Finally, don't be afraid to take a decision and stand by it. Being prepared to fail – and learn from failure – is an essential characteristic of Agile methodology. And in times of uncertainty, your colleagues might be afraid to commit to an untested course of action. So be bold, step into a power vacuum with a decision and be prepared that if you make the wrong call, you will need to iterate and try again, honestly and transparently.

Wherever you find colleagues with these competencies, you should be able to identify the people who are likely to be your most enthusiastic supporters and persuade them to become advocates for change. Even with their networks and relationships, they won't be able to convince everyone, but the more of them you get on board, the easier your job will become.

The changemakers to look out for

I cannot overstate the value of communities and networks here. Everyone I speak to about embedding digital culture – regardless of what type or size of business they are in – talks about the challenges of skills, talents and information being locked in silos. By building in opportunities for knowledge-sharing, your people can benefit from peer-to-peer learning, finding others who are having similar experiences and helping to pull each other along on the journey.

As soon as you build those networks, digital adoption can begin to amplify. Here are some of the personae you can look for inside your own organisation:

Pioneers

Pioneers are the people who get it. They are usually younger members of the team in junior roles: digital natives who were born in a world of touch screens, virtual engagement and seamless app interfaces. They spend a considerable amount of their lives online and a digital mindset feels intuitive for them. Their ability to experiment hasn't been polluted by years of corporate risk-aversion, they are willing to learn and they expect to make a difference in their working lives. Their wide-eyed enthusiasm, if harnessed properly, can energise others in the workplace and help carry them along on the journey to data innovation.

However, these same colleagues might not understand how new knowledge and ideas can be operationalised across the business, they are unlikely to have a wider view of how their role can feed into an organisational strategy and they may lack influence and executive presence, failing to be taken seriously by senior leaders.

Enablers

Enablers are influencers. Often senior executives or board members, they tend to have some budgetary control, holding purse-strings they may not realise can be used to advance the data innovation agenda. They may be very experienced domain experts in a particular business function and their widespread influence across the organisation can open doors. This makes them well placed to sponsor initiatives, mentor high-potential talent, make useful connections and introduce problem-owners to solution-creators.

That said, they may not have any technical expertise, or understand the opportunities that data innovation can offer, which could be an obstacle to them being able to progress projects. They are likely to be time-poor and focused on other priorities, like compliance, risk or operational efficiency, so communicating value to them needs to be clear and concise, as their sponsorship is key to success.

PA Consulting calls these 'halo leaders': 'These are your star managers and thought leaders with a great track record, who are widely respected and supported. These leaders are the cultural architects of organisational agility. They're able to deal with ambiguity and lead with empathy. They have the emotional intelligence to address concerns on the ground and consistently promote a culture of continuous learning and innovation.'

Practitioners

Practitioners are often subject matter experts or technical specialists. They are the ones who have the expertise you need to disseminate through the business, but may feel frustrated. They need to understand the gap that exists in order to make them better mentors, better digital leaders.

Practitioners are the people who can take change forward, but they need the enthusiasm of the Pioneers to provide them with courage and they need the influence of the Enablers to open the doors.

Understanding the value that each of these people can bring to the table, and creating a space for them to explore possibility together, is essential in driving forward transformational data innovation in your organisation.

Space to learn and grow

'Organisations that put humans at the centre of their transformation are 2.6 times more likely to succeed than those that do not'

EY, 2022

Appreciating the vast difference between learning styles is critical to your success. We all have our own approaches to personal learning and development. So, use the Periodic Table of Data Strategy Elements to create a space to inspire, to talk about what failed, what worked and why.

Build in time and space to learn, identify skills gaps and encourage people to find the pathways to development that work for them.

And most importantly, enable your people to collaborate, to ensure that growth and discussion is cross-functional, bringing in different viewpoints and lessons learned.

A lot of the coaching and training work I do with organisations is about creating the psychological safe space to explore a topic, to admit that – not only do we not always know the answers – but we don't necessarily understand the right questions. Removing the fear of failure, judgement and retribution can quite suddenly expand people's horizons as to what is possible. This is about asking people, 'What do you bring to the game and how can we help you use that?'

It is really important to understand that the problems you can see in one department or function may also exist in others, but rise to the surface in different ways. And until you have those open conversations, you won't realise that the fix is already in the room.

Data culture needs to find a place at the heart of everything you do. More often than not, the thing that prevents digital transformation is the cultural roadblocks. Cultural readiness programmes are shown to significantly reduce the high failure rate affecting most digital transformations.

The legacy challenges with systems, processes, infrastructure, mindset and capability found within most businesses are all very real. The capabilities and skills you can build are transferrable and can de-risk your journey by providing teams with the cultural building blocks they will need to be successful.

For most businesses, these recommendations involve activities they're already doing – but the importance of a singular vision and consistency of message cannot be understated.

Introducing the Data Success Framework

Tapping in to decades of domain and technical expertise by working closely with a group of CTOs, CIOs and senior (non-technology) leaders over the last year, all of whom have led major corporate transformation programmes, I have developed a framework for success, outlined below.

The foundations for this are in the research I conducted with more than 300 companies, but the group of senior executives who so kindly contributed their time and expertise to workshop this framework are the real stars of the show. These leaders have experience in nine of our ten market segments and between them had been involved in 23 organisational change programmes. While only a handful of those could be described as astonishingly successful (by the participants' own admission), the lessons learned along the way proved invaluable in determining what not to do, as much as in recognising the actions and behaviours that are required for a successful data transformation.

In the workshops, we began with 38 possible measures for success, based on the qualitative and quantitative research

data, and worked to refine them into ten key actions, tested for robustness against real-world transformation challenges, which the participants agreed could be incorporated into a comprehensive data strategy in any of their businesses and – crucially – could be added to the objectives and KPIs of employees and leadership to ensure the widespread adoption of organisational change.

The ten actions are categorised in three overall areas of responsibility: Leading, Collaborating and Learning.

Leading

Every CEO, board and executive team has a responsibility to build and safeguard a long-term future for their organisation, so succession planning is an integral part of any business's continuity plan. Therefore, the first four actions in the framework are ones that leadership must embrace for a transformation programme to thrive across an organisation, but they also demonstrate the leadership behaviours that we need to look for, identify and celebrate, in order to work out who in the business has the potential to rise and replace the existing cohort of leaders.

To refer back to the *Barriers to Digital Transformation* study, the majority of CTOs, CIOs and technology leaders agreed that 'leading with empathy and kindness' was the most likely indicator of a successful change programme. This obviously applies to CEOs but is also the trait we should all be on the lookout for at every level of an organisation. All four of the 'Leading' actions are components of empathetic leadership.

Inspiring change

'Leaders are trusted to communicate the organisation's strategy and motivate and inspire people to embrace technology to deliver it.'

Recognising the need for change, and being prepared to shine a light on the way forward is an essential trait for leadership in digital-first organisations. Change is unsettling, for all the reasons already discussed, but knowing that the demand signals for transformation come from the top will make the transition from one state to another a part of the culture of a business. Consistently communicating the need for change, explaining why it is important, how long it will take and what it will involve, provides employees with the same roadmap as their colleagues. Even if it feels uncertain, knowing that the rest of our team is in the same boat will minimise the anxiety surrounding the programme.

One of the most destabilising factors in communicating about transformation is a sense of division, where some members of staff feel that others in more privileged (and presumably 'safer') positions have greater access to relevant information. Ensuring that messages are delivered in the same way at the same time helps to level that playing field and engender trust in both the process and the leaders driving it.

Leading with integrity

'Senior leaders and board members lead from a place of insight, having developed the digital skills and mindset to drive forward the organisation's future.'

You can ask people to follow you into the unknown all you like, but if you're not prepared to take your own medicine, it will completely undermine and destabilise your efforts. In order to lead a transformation, the panel of experts involved in the workshops all agreed that leading with integrity is a major key to success. It is not enough for leaders instruct their employees to develop a digital mindset, if they're not prepared to live those values themselves and demonstrate the importance of being open to change and being prepared to admit they don't know what they don't know.

Building digital culture

'Everyone, at every level, works to ensure the organisation uses technology safely, securely and strategically and they have the courage and support to challenge anyone who isn't doing the same.'

Building a digital culture brings in the elements of Embedding Data Innovation Behaviours: fostering collaboration, exploring possibility together, engaging, empowering being responsive to new information and taking risks. These apply across the organisation, but they must be seen in leadership for meaningful change to take place. This action is about building a safe space for innovation to flourish, and that permission needs to come from the top.

Including people

'Diversity of thought, expertise and approach is valued, so people can trust in the integrity of the organisation's data-driven technologies.'

Any moves towards Agile and Lean behaviours as part of adopting a digital mindset will necessarily help to flatten rigid hierarchical structures, which also means progressing away from traditional 'command-and-control' ways of communicating. The emphasis on collaboration at every level requires those with the greatest power in an organisation to cede some of their control of the situation to those they work with, allowing for a greater variety of voices to contribute to overall decision-making.

As discussed in the Periodic table, diversity, equity and inclusion is critical to having faith in the ethics and integrity of your data and processes, and therefore to understanding data as a strategic asset within the business.

Collaborating

The next three actions are about purposefully improving the way teams work together and can be easily added to individual team KPIs and metrics, to support the development of a data culture throughout an organisation.

Embedding data strategy

'People at all levels understand how data strategy supports the organisation's objectives and are able to communicate their role in driving it forward.'

Elevating the data strategy to ensure it is discussed at board level, included in annual reports and discussed openly in team or town hall meetings is essential to demystifying what in many companies can appear to be an obscure 'dark art'. Shining light on it and making sure it is discussed more transparently will make the concept of a data strategy far more accessible – especially to those who have no technology background or experience.

First, though, leaders need to ensure it is aligned to the overall corporate strategy, so that it is easy for people to see how a digital success can be translated into meeting wider company targets, like productivity, financial success or opportunities for growth and development.

Rewarding digital mindset

'The company appraises, recognises and rewards digital-first behaviours which support activities driving the organisation forward. People are motivated to do their best work, together.'

By factoring digital mindset attributes and data innovation behaviours into personal objectives, employees will be able to clearly understand their contributions to building a more cohesive, collaborative, digital-first workplace. Remember the adage that people don't have to *do* digital to *be* digital. By selectively aligning elements with job types, it is possible to ensure that every member of a team picks up – and is held accountable for – adopting some of the elements the team needs to be successful. This also means that, as a business, you can begin to reward the behaviours that add the most value through the regular appraisal process, encouraging team members to play their part.

Enabling innovation

'Each role is designed to encourage open collaboration with others so that new ways of working can be discovered and deployed.'

By including digital mindset and data innovation behaviours into team or departmental objectives, it will fall to line-managers to begin embedding those into existing objectives, as well as into new roles as they are created organically. Make it clear to hiring managers and HR teams that every time a new role is created, there is an opportunity to bring in new collaborators, with different approaches, viewpoints and experiences, rather than hiring a cookie cutter replacement of the last person in the role. Actively working to encourage open collaboration has become an essential characteristic of most businesses post-Covid, where many workplace environments are now flexible or hybrid to some degree, so collaboration is rapidly becoming a natural part of the DNA of many organisations.

Learning

The final three sections are designed to encourage and reinforce data innovation behaviours, ensuring business resilience to change by continually developing both technical and non-technical talent.

Developing capability

'Leaders support their people to learn and grow, ensuring they have access to the tools and expertise they need to thrive. The organisation appoints the right people, at the right time, for the right roles.'

Whether your people learn in groups or source their mandatory training through a work-provided learning management system (LMS), most companies have some sort of education protocol in place to support their employees' ongoing professional development. Try to make sure the programmes in place reinforce digital mindset learning, by using the Periodic Table as a baseline, but the key is to encourage (and reward) curiosity and an enthusiasm for lifelong learning.

The second piece of this puzzle was the cause of some discussion in the workshops because it is all too often overlooked by busy professionals: appointing the right people, at the right time, for the right roles. Because of pressures of timing, funding or other priorities shifting, far too many businesses fail to fill their employment gaps in a timely fashion, putting other team members under strain to 'cope', which can have a profound impact on everyone's ability to meet their (and your) objectives. How many times have you witnessed a colleague resigning from a role, only for their position to wait weeks to be approved and re-advertised, possibly meaning months before the role is filled?

Also, keep an eye on those 'changemakers' in the organisation: if you have identified a Pioneer or a Practitioner who could add more value to the organisation in a broader role, try to work out how you can help them grow their influence and responsibilities, to increase their impact and celebrate their development.

It is also important to consider which skills you have a chance to bring in to your team when it comes to hiring replacement staff: every time a vacancy becomes available, use the opportunity to think about whether you really need a like-for-like replacement, or whether the skills gap in your team is still the same shape as the person who left it.

Promoting lifelong learning

'The organisation provides leaders and people with opportunities to grow and learn, from within their industry and elsewhere. And to share new insights and knowledge with colleagues to inspire change and growth.'

The beauty of creating a truly collaborative environment is the opportunity this provides for cross-pollination of knowledge. When one member of a team fully grasps one of the elements from the Periodic Table, encourage them to share their learning and insights with others. By enabling enthusiasm for learning and development to spread, you can plant seeds of innovation all over the place. Give your people time, not just to learn by themselves, but to share what they have learned with others. You can propagate this through networks and communities, but you can also do very simple things, like asking a colleague to share her experience with your team about why a project failed and what she learned from it.

Embracing data ethics

'People at all levels are encouraged to understand how the organisation collects and uses data, and they are empowered to challenge biases.'

The holy grail of data innovation is for people who do not consider themselves to be in digital roles to be able to discuss data strategy fluently with others. Data ethics may seem complex from the outside, but in reality, it is about understanding the 'why' of data and how it connects to your purpose as a business and as an employer.

If a member of your team can feel comfortable discussing what they know about the way your organisation collects and uses data, they will also be able to identify why this matches with their values (or flag up concerns if it does not). This is not just about giving them the freedom to challenge biases or problems in your data collection, storage and use, but about asking them to constantly find ways to improve how your organisation *behaves* when it comes to data strategy.

In summary...

All ten of these actions are easy to understand, simple to put into practice and needn't cost a penny to implement. All they take is time, determination and willingness to transform together.

That isn't to say they will make transformation easy. Change is hard and unsettling for workers, who will bring with them all manner of psychological baggage, personal motivations and needs, and they will probably all start from different places and move at different speeds. That's humans for you.

Organisations are varied too. You may look at this list and believe you have a long journey ahead of you, or you might believe you already do most or all the actions in the framework, so you're nearly there. But these actions need to carried out with intent, with a transformation programme in mind.

The good news is you can be a successful transformation leader if you believe you can:

- Inspire change
- Lead with integrity
- Build digital culture
- Include people
- Embed data strategy
- Reward digital mindset
- Enable innovation
- Develop capability
- Promote lifelong learning
- Embrace data ethics

This framework provides a set of flexible principles which our group of experts agreed can be applied in the world's most complex business environments, and we believe they should also work in much smaller operations too.

Conclusions

Let me be explicitly clear: digital transformation is everybody's job. If you're in an organisation going through a change programme and you don't like it, you have a choice: move jobs or play a proactive part in making your transformation better. It's a Hobson's Choice, really, as there is only one productive option: if you move to another company and they're not also going through some sort of transformation, then they just haven't started it yet.

As I said at the outset, this isn't a book about technology, it's a book about people. Artificial intelligence is going to fundamentally change the world of work. No one knows exactly how – trust me, I've spoken to and worked with some of the world's leading experts, and they haven't got a Scooby Doo – but it will. Its impacts will be felt in many ways, in every company, in varying timeframes. Some roles will be eradicated completely, some barely touched, but it will be felt across every economy in the world. AI is only the latest technological innovation to upend the dynamics of the workplace, but it is the most universal change since every desk got a PC in the 1990s.

Change is inevitable. Businesses have been transforming for the last few decades. And the rapid adoption of AI and other general purpose technologies will continue to accelerate the rate of transformation for decades to come.

So make yours better. Lean in to it, adopt a digital mindset and open your eyes to what you can learn in the process. If you're not part of the solution, I'm afraid you are almost certainly part of the problem.

I really hope you find this book helpful. I'm not some lofty academic looking down at corporate culture from 30,000 feet and dropping logic bombs: I'm someone who has spent 25 years at every level in a number of different corporate cultures, trying to improve them from the inside. My intention is that the advice dispensed in these pages is as practical and applicable as possible to real world situations.

Whatever the ambition, scope or scale of your transformation, whether you're using artificial intelligence to revolutionise the way you manufacture components, or using smart contracts on a blockchain to ensure ethical principles in your supply chain, or launching your first foray into e-commerce, technology is rarely the biggest challenge. It is almost always the humans in your loop.

People don't usually fear change itself: that would be irrational. However, they do fear what they can rationalise, which is the perceived impacts of that change on the way they work, the future of their jobs, the likelihood of them being punished for failure, their financial security, their ability to find enjoyment in the activities they spend their days doing.

Every human relationship, whether that's with a friend, a spouse or an employer, is transactional. Good relationships are ones where the participants have negotiated an acceptable balance between pleasure and pain, between risk and reward. Toxic relationships are merely situations where an acceptable balance hasn't been negotiated successfully.

Psychological safety in an organisational setting is so hard to manage, precisely because it involves so many interdependent relationships, and most employees learn to lower their expectations, as they don't have sufficient leverage to successfully negotiate acceptable compromises across all their working relationships. The employer has disproportionate level of power in this equation, so it falls to CEOs, team leaders, line managers and senior executives to create opportunities for people to explore their potential.

Because change involves the unknown and is being inflicted on workers from above, it is impossible for them to know whether pleasure will outweigh the pain. Which is why it can only succeed if they feel the benefits might outweigh the risks.

Remember, 'leading with empathy and kindness' is the number one indicator of a successful transformation. If you take away only one thing from this book, it's that this doesn't just apply to CEOs. Leadership can take many forms and change always creates opportunities that never existed before. In times of uncertainty, your colleagues will be desperately on the lookout for people they can trust and depend on. Be that person. Lead with empathy and be kind to each other. My most robust, trusted friendships have been forged in challenging times: we are people who have gotten each other out of scrapes, buoyed each other in the storm and depended on each other to handle struggles together.

Research notes & methodology

Interviews

92 expert interviews were conducted online or in person between 9 May and 14 September 2023:

Nature of engagement	Dates	Approx average size of UK entity	Sectors included
22 interviews with senior innovation, change and transformation leaders about implementing digital culture change in large businesses	9 - 30 May 2023	17,900 FTE	Banking, Insurance, Manufacturing, Minerals, Energy, Utilities, Healthcare, Legal, FMCG, Retail, Infrastructure, Technology, Media
17 interviews with CTOs, CIOs and CDOs in major global corporates about challenges implementing SaaS solutions at-scale	1 - 16 June 2023	26,800 FTE	Banking, Defence, Electrical, Manufacturing, Engineering, Energy, Utilities, Chemical, Pharma, Medical Devices, Consumer Goods, Legal, Professional Services
16 interviews with Non Exec Directors, Company Secretaries, Chairs, Board Advisors and Management Consultants about executive data literacy	28 June - 20 July 2023	12,300 FTE	Automotive, Transport, Shipping, Manufacturing, Engineering, Energy, Pharma, Legal, Technology, Healthcare, Hospitality, Facilities Management

Nature of engagement	Dates	Approx average size of UK entity	Sectors included
11 interviews with governance professionals and management consultants about trends in management information & Board reporting	1 - 21 August 2023	37,300 FTE	Professional Services, Manufacturing, Banking, Technology
26 interviews with senior executives (Heads of, VPs, Directors & C-Suite) about corporate AI, machine learning and data science capabilities	15 August - 14 September 2023	14,600 FTE	Banking, Insurance, Pharma, Medical Devices, Precision Tooling, Engineering, Shipping, Manufacturing, Logistics, Energy, Utilities, Healthcare, Legal, FMCG, Retail, Professional Services

Round tables

23 participants took part in three expert round tables between 21 June and 26 July 2023:

Nature of engagement	Dates	Approx average size of UK entity	Sectors included
Digital Talent & Skills, London (8 attendees)	21 June 2023	11,200 FTE	Automotive, Engineering, Energy, Technology
Data: Risk and Reporting, London (7 attendees)	12 July 2023	3,700 FTE	Professional Services, Legal, Banking
Applied AI vs. ChatGPT, London (8 attendees)	26 July 2023	4,600 FTE	Healthcare, Pharma, Defence, Professional Services

Recording methodology

Conversations were audio-recorded and transcribed where permission was given in 73 of the 92 expert interviews. In the remaining 19 interviews, notes were made on the calls and fuller notes written up within 24 hours. None of the round tables were recorded, but conversational notes were written up and shared with all participants within 48 hours and no corrections were received. All interviews and round tables were held under the Chatham House rule with agreement that no attribution of comments would be made in subsequent publications.

Surveys

234 leaders were polled in three online industry surveys between 18 May and 10 September 2023:

Nature of engagement	Dates
105 Board members and senior executives (Heads of, VPs, Directors & C-Suite) surveyed about interpreting management information and ESG data within their businesses	18 May - 15 June 2023
38 CIOs, CTOs & AI Directors in enterprise-scale businesses polled about the risks and barriers around digital transformation	4 - 25 June 2023
91 senior leaders (CEO, Chair, Board, C-Suite, Director, Head of) surveyed about corporate AI capabilities in large businesses	1 August - 10 September 2023

Methodology weighting, biases and caveats

1. **Age of companies**

   Preliminary market research and a meta-review of existing literature found that the 400 largest employers collectively employ 8.11m people in the UK. On average, they are 107 years old and employ 28,613 people, based on data from company websites, company reports, Companies House and the UK Department of Work and Pensions. Outreach was targeted on the 89% of businesses which are older than the internet, pre-dating the year 2000 CE. This has led to a greater weighting of engagement across interviews and surveys from old-world industrial and services businesses (with notably high response rates from manufacturing and banking sectors), while there was lower engagement with younger companies (particularly in the technology, media and telecoms sectors).

2. Size of companies

Research focused on enterprise-scale challenges with digital culture and technology adoption, so there was limited engagement from businesses with smaller employee footprints. This does mean that of the 234 companies to have participated in some way, fewer than 10% of the overall sample size is from companies with fewer than 1,000 FTE employees. Responses from this limited sample suggest cultural interventions and training designed for Enterprise firms would also be beneficial for companies in the large, but pre-enterprise (250–1,000 FTE) category.

3. Context

The author made every effort to ensure that quotes and comments have only been used faithfully and contextually. Each of the structured interviews considered 10–12 questions which could be provided in advance to participants if requested. However, with the nature of conversational interviews, some of the verbatim responses to particular questions also proved relevant to others, and in some cases, interviewees chose to explore other, related topics, which were also noted and used in commentary.

4. Geography

The roundtables and workshops took place in London, UK; to best knowledge, 84 of the 92 interviewees were in the UK at the time of the in-person or virtual interview, although several participants had remits broader than just the UK; IP addresses of survey respondents were not tracked, but given that the outreach and questions were UK-focused, it is assumed the majority of respondents were UK-domiciled and/or working for principally UK-headquartered companies and/or working in the UK entities of global organisations.

5. Sectoral representation

Across the research, most market segments are well represented, with responses from industrial and services businesses in relatively equal measure. However, within the industrial space, there was a low response rate (or declines to be interviewed) from construction and infrastructure firms, while in the services space, there was limited engagement with technology, media and telecoms businesses. While their responses are included in aggregated data, there are not sufficient sample sizes for detailed analyses of those sectors.

Breakdown of survey respondents (n.234)

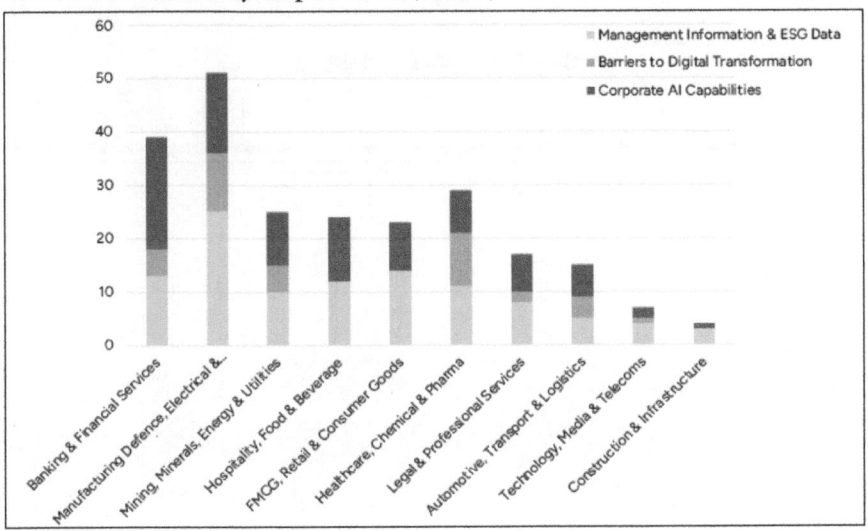

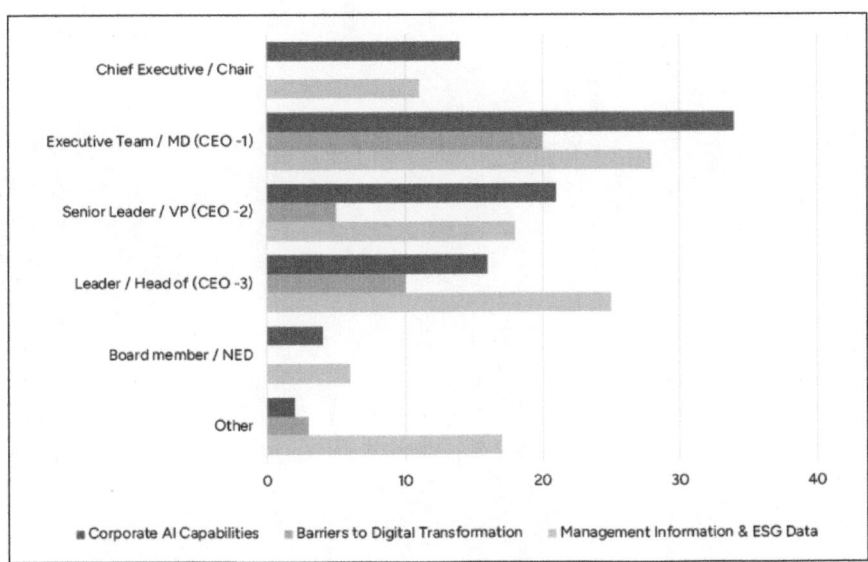

Data Culture

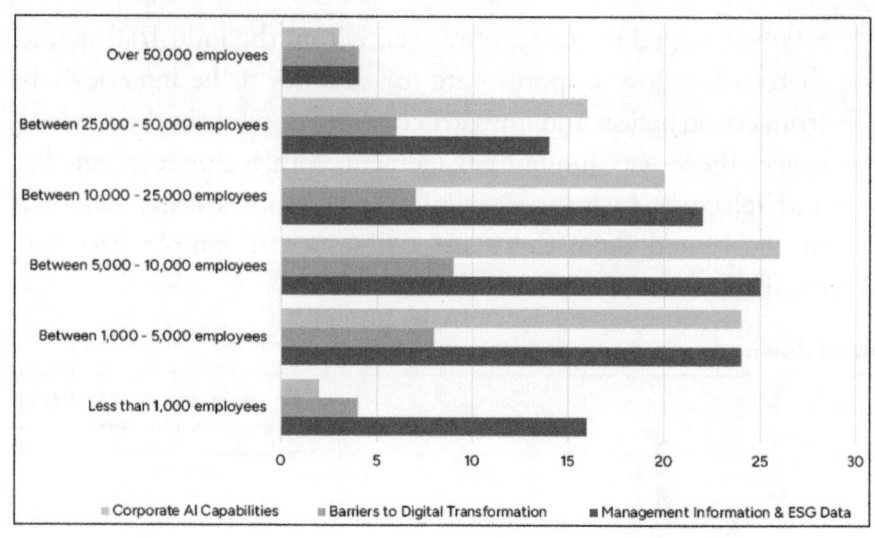

Acknowledgements

To the hundreds of survey respondents and the 92 interviewees who so willingly shared their time and expertise. I learned more from you in just a few months than I ever thought possible.

To the dozen inspiring experts who helped to develop the Periodic Table and the Data Success Framework. I would love to name you all, but I did promise anonymity and the results of our work together are exponentially better because of your honesty and candour. You really made me take my own medicine when it came to the Elements of (12) Lifelong Learning, (13) Fostering Collaboration and (14) Building Networks and Communities.

To Michella, my sometime 'work wife' and co-conspirator, thank you for dragging me to New York to think, for nudging me on and helping me to (15) Explore Possibility Together and to (19) Be Braver and Bolder.

To my wonderful advisors, Caroline, Rakhi, Mike and Becca: your generosity and insight provided me with the psychological safety net I needed to (24) Fail Fast, (25) Learn through Feedback Loops and (26) Iterate Better Solutions.

To Manisha, also an invaluable advisor and sometime 'work wife', so many of the principles featured in this book have foundations in your pioneering work and the things that you taught me – not least conceptualising the Elements as a

Periodic Table. I owe you a profound debt of gratitude for your (3) Humility and EQ and for (16) Sharing Ideas and Good Practices with me.

To Pieter, my biggest cheerleader, whose winning combination of intellectual challenge and unwavering belief in me made me feel safe enough to (1) Embrace the Unknown.

To Sam and Archie, I really couldn't have done any of this without your help and support in devising and supervising such an epic research project: your patience, guidance and 'left-brained brilliance' taught me how to (18) Use Data to Drive Decision Making.

To Connor, Nikki, Steve, Elle-Jay, Amelia and the whole team at Icon Books, thank you for (23) Taking a Risk on me and all your help and support.

To Christopher, Stevo, Nick, Kirstie, Devina, Linsey, Huss, Fiona, Josephine, Julie and my mum and dad: thanks for being in my corner, giving me advice, puffing me up when it got a bit tough and grounding me when I got a bit high on my own fumes. I keep learning from all of you and I'm grateful to have you around.

Vaily x

References

Chapter 1

1. https://www.bcg.com/publications/2020/increasing-odds-of-success-in-digital-transformation
2. https://www.gov.uk/government/statistics/business-population-estimates-2021/business-population-estimates-for-the-uk-and-regions-2021-statistical-release-html

Chapter 2

1. https://sloanreview.mit.edu/article/why-manufacturers-need-a-phased-approach-to-digital-transformation/
2. Our Waste, Our Resources: A Strategy for England (HM Government, 2018)
3. https://www.theguardian.com/environment/2024/apr/04/just-57-companies-linked-to-80-of-greenhouse-gas-emissions-since-2016?ref=newsletters.holoniq.com
4. Network Thinking: The paradigm shift in understanding industrial supply chains (R² Factory, January 2023)
5. https://www.newyorkfed.org/research/policy/gscpi#/overview
6. https://www.nashsquared.com/dlr-2022
7. https://www.netwrix.com/2022_cloud_data_security_report.html
8. https://www.absolutemarketsinsights.com

Chapter 3

1. https://www.bbc.com/worklife/article/20211022-why-were-so-terrified-of-the-unknown
2. Jon Ronson (2011), The Psychopath Test: A Journey Through the Madness Industry (Picador)
3. https://www.bcg.com/publications/2018/how-diverse-leadership-teams-boost-innovation
4. https://www.glassdoor.com/blog/glassdoors-diversity-and-inclusion-workplace-survey/
5. https://www.mckinsey.com/featured-insights/diversity-and-inclusion/diversity-wins-how-inclusion-matters
6. https://ftsewomenleaders.com/wp-content/uploads/2023/03/ftse-women-leaders-review-report-2022-v2.pdf
7. https://www.gov.uk/government/publications/ethnic-diversity-of-uk-boards-the-parker-review
8. https://wbdirectors.co.uk/wp-content/uploads/2024/06/Hidden-Truth-2024-Fullreport.pdf
9. https://pubsonline.informs.org/doi/10.1287/orsc.2021.15132
10. https://www.amazon.co.uk/Guide-Events-Everything-brilliant-corporate-ebook/dp/B076DLC1GD

Chapter 4

1. https://blogs.microsoft.com/on-the-issues/2023/07/21/commitment-safe-secure-ai/
2. https://openai.com/blog/frontier-model-forum
3. https://arxiv.org/abs/2001.03246 (2021)
4. https://aiindex.stanford.edu/wp-content/uploads/2024/05/HAI_AI-Index-Report-2024.pdf
5. https://jameswphillips.substack.com/p/s-and-t-is-the-uk-a-world-leader
6. https://www.cbinsights.com/research/report/top-acquirers-artificial-intelligence/ (2021)

7. https://www.globaldata.com/media/technology/nhs-federated-data-platform-contract-quadruple-palantirs-uk-public-sector-revenue-says-globaldata/
8. https://quartr.com/insights/company-research/the-rise-of-google-meta-amazon-and-youtube-in-advertising
9. https://www.fortunebusinessinsights.com/industry-reports/artificial-intelligence-market-100114
10. https://www.nber.org/papers/w25148 (2018)
11. https://www.cnbc.com/2024/02/19/magnificent-7-profits-now-exceed-almost-every-country-in-the-world-should-we-be-worried.html
12. https://www.morganstanley.com/im/publication/insights/articles/article_stockmarketconcentration.pdf
13. https://www.gov.uk/government/publications/intellectual-property-and-investment-in-artificial-intelligence/intellectual-property-and-investment-in-artificial-intelligence (2022)
14. https://www.idc.com/getdoc.jsp?containerId=US49018922

Chapter 5

1. https://www.ons.gov.uk/employmentandlabourmarket/peopleinwork/employmentandemployeetypes/adhocs/12467employmentbyageindustryandoccupationuk201020 15and2019
2. https://www.mckinsey.com/capabilities/operations/our-insights/adopting-ai-at-speed-and-scale-the-4ir-push-to-stay-competitive
3. https://www.gov.uk/government/publications/ai-regulation-a-pro-innovation-approach
4. https://www.stateof.ai/
5. https://artificialintelligenceact.eu/ai-act-explorer
6. https://www.whitehouse.gov/ostp/ai-bill-of-rights/

7. https://www.whitehouse.gov/wp-content/uploads/2023/05/National-Artificial-Intelligence-Research-and-Development-Strategic-Plan-2023-Update.pdf
8. https://arxiv.org/pdf/2401.05749
9. https://www.nature.com/articles/s41586-024-07566-y
10. https://pro.morningconsult.com/analyst-reports/h2-2023-geopolitical-risk-report-trust-governance
11. https://cdn.openai.com/papers/sparse-autoencoders.pdf
12. https://appraisenetwork.ai/research/mp-survey-2023
13. https://institute.global/insights/politics-and-governance/new-national-purpose-ai-promises-world-leading-future-of-britain
14. https://www.ipsos.com/sites/default/files/ct/news/documents/2023-07/ipsos-ai-in-the-workplace-uk-charts.pdf
15. https://www.cliffordchance.com/hubs/tech-group-hub/tech-group/our-relationship-with-ai-friend-or-foe.html
16. https://www.turing.ac.uk/news/no-evidence-ai-disinformation-or-deepfakes-impacted-uk-french-or-european-elections-results
17. https://assets.ey.com/content/dam/ey-sites/ey-com/en_gl/topics/long-term-value/ey-europe-long-term-value-and-corporate-governance-survey-march-2024-v2.pdf
18. http://arxiv.org/pdf/2311.16863
19. https://arxiv.org/pdf/2211.02001
20. https://www.gstatic.com/gumdrop/sustainability/google-2024-environmental-report.pdf
21. https://www.wsj.com/business/energy-oil/tech-industry-wants-to-lock-up-nuclear-power-for-ai-6cb75316
22. https://www.theguardian.com/technology/article/2024/jul/02/google-ai-emissions
23. https://www.gov.uk/government/publications/ai-activity-in-uk-businesses/ai-activity-in-uk-businesses-executive-summary
24. https://www.gartner.com/en/newsroom/press-releases/2022-08-22-gartner-survey-reveals-80-percent-of-executives-think-automation-can-be-applied-to-any-business-decision (2022)

25. https://www.ey.com/en_gl/consulting/tech-horizon-survey(2022)
26. https://assets.publishing.service.gov.uk/media/6711176 c386bf0964853d747/industrial-strategy-green-paper.pdf
27. https://www3.weforum.org/docs/WEF_National_AI_ Strategy.pdf (2019)
28. https://www.mckinsey.com/~/media/mckinsey/featured%20 insights/artificial%20intelligence/notes%20from%20the%20 ai%20frontier%20applications%20and%20value%20 of%20deep%20learning/notes-from-the-ai-frontier-insights-from-hundreds-of-use-cases-discussion-paper.ashx (2018)
29. https://www.institute.global/insights/ politics-and-governance/new-national-purpose-innovation-can-power-future-britain (2023)
30. https://www.oxfordinsights.com/ai-readiness (2023)
31. https://www.gov.uk/government/publications/ ai-safety-summit-2023-the-bletchley-declaration/ the-bletchley-declaration-by-countries-attending-the-ai-safety-summit-1-2-november-2023
32. https://www.stateof.ai/
33. https://papers.ssrn.com/sol3/papers.cfm?abstract_ id=3144563 (2018)
34. https://www.governance.ai/research-paper/agenda (2017)

Chapter 6

1. https://newsroom.accenture.com/news/accenture-technology-vision-2023-generative-ai-to-usher-in-a-bold-new-future-for-business-merging-physical-and-digital-worlds.htm (2023)
2. https://www.alixpartners.com/media-center/press-releases/2023-disruption-index-report/ (2022)
3. https://www.ey.com/en_gl/newsroom/2024/06/82-percent-of-european-financial-services-boardrooms-include-directors-with-political-experience-helping-the-sector-navigate-the-2024-election-super-cycle-and-ongoing-geopolitical-uncertainty

Chapter 7

1. https://www.mckinsey.com/capabilities/mckinsey-digital/our-insights/the-economic-potential-of-generative-ai-the-next-productivity-frontier (2023)
2. https://www.pewresearch.org/social-trends/2023/07/26/which-u-s-workers-are-more-exposed-to-ai-on-their-jobs/ (2023)
3. https://www.mckinsey.com/mgi/our-research/generative-ai-and-the-future-of-work-in-america (2023)
4. https://futuredotnow.uk/about-us/the-hidden-middle (2023)
5. https://kpmg.com/xx/en/home/insights/2022/09/kpmg-global-tech-report-2022.html (2022)
6. https://www.goldmansachs.com/intelligence/pages/generative-ai-could-raise-global-gdp-by-7-percent.html
7. https://www.cognizant.com/no/en/insights/blog/articles/new-study-gen-ai-could-affect-90-percent-of-all-jobs
8. https://www.nber.org/system/files/working_papers/w30389/w30389.pdf
9. Mo Gawdat (2021), Scary Smart (Bluebird Books)

Chapter 8

1. https://www.researchgate.net/profile/John-Ward-5/publication/272484960_Success_and_Failure_in_Transformation_Lessons_from_13_Case_Studies/links/5746c93708ae9f741b43b049/Success-and-Failure-in-Transformation-Lessons-from-13-Case-Studies.pdf
2. https://www.elgaronline.com/edcollchap/edcoll/9781781000892/9781781000892.00007.xml
3. Carole Dweck (2016), Mindset: The New Psychology of Success (Ballantyne Books)
4. https://en.wikipedia.org/wiki/Parkinson%27s_law
5. https://www.interaction-design.org/literature/topics/design-thinking

6. https://www.paconsulting.com/global-shifts/ future-organisations/organisational-agility

7. https://www.mckinsey.com/~/media/mckinsey/business%20 functions/people%20and%20organizational%20 performance/our%20insights/leading%20agile%20 transformation%20the%20new%20capabilities%20 leaders%20need%20to%20build/leading-agile- transformation-the-new-capabilities-leaders-need-to-build- 21st-century-organizations.pdf

8. https://books.google.co.uk/books?hl=en&lr=&id=ALO3d3Y rG4oC&oi=fnd&pg=PP1&dq=fook+white+gardner+2006 &ots=DwLHNjJ_wB&sig=KhxAJ5UBa1oIBzTolP011B7v B5E#v=onepage&q=fook%20white%20gardner%202006

9. Helen Storey and Mathilda Marie Joubert (2004), The Emotional Dance of Creative Collaboration, Collaborative Creativity: Contemporary Perspectives.